THROW LIKE A
Girl

Measurement Conversion Information

To determine the metric equivalents for the U.S. measurements that appear in the text of this book, use the following conversion factors:

1 inch = 2.54 centimeters (cm)

1 foot = 0.3048 meter (m)

1 yard = 0.9144 meter (m)

1 mile = 1.609 kilometers (km)

1 cup (liquid) = 240 milliliters (ml)

1 ounce (liquid) = 30 ml

1 ounce = 28.33 grams (g)

1 pound = 0.4536 kilogram (kg)

For a free color catalog describing Gareth Stevens' list of high-quality books and multimedia programs, call 1-800-542-2595 (USA) or 1-800-461-9120 (Canada). Gareth Stevens Publishing's Fax: (414) 332-3567.

Library of Congress Cataloging-in-Publication Data available upon request from publisher. Fax: (414) 332-3567 for the attention of the Publishing Records Department.

ISBN 0-8368-2674-4

This North American edition first published in 2000 by
Gareth Stevens Publishing
A World Almanac Education Group Company
330 West Olive Street, Suite 100
Milwaukee, WI 53212 USA

This edition © 2000 by Gareth Stevens, Inc. Original edition published in 2000 by Beyond Words Publishing, Inc., 20827 NW Cornell Road, Suite 500, Hillsboro, OR 97124. Original edition © 2000 by Beyond Words Publishing, Inc. Additional end matter © 2000 by Gareth Stevens, Inc.

Editor: Barbara Mann
Cover design: Marci Doane Roth
Interior book design: Brad King and Susan Shankin
Composition: William H. Brunson Typography Services
Gareth Stevens editors: Dorothy L. Gibbs and Ann Angel
Editorial assistant: Diane Laska-Swanke

Every effort has been made to contact the copyright owners of the photographs and illustrations in this book. Any copyright owner who has not been contacted should write to the original publisher, Beyond Words Publishing, Inc., Hillsboro, OR. The publishers gratefully acknowledge and thank the following for their generous assistance and permission to use photos and illustrations:

Illustration Credits
Food Pyramid: Courtesy of United States Department of Agriculture

Photo Credits
Sarah Gebhardt: Courtesy of Mysterioso®
Cammi Granato: Courtesy of USA Hockey
Donna Lopiano: Photograph by Beth Green Studios
Kathryn Reith: Photograph by Beth Green Studios
Jade Smalls: Photograph by David Bartley
Sheryl Swoopes: Courtesy of Octagon Athlete Representation
Lesley Visser: ABC Photography Department

The information contained in this book is intended to be educational and not for diagnosis, prescription, or treatment of mental and/or physical health disorders, whatsoever. This information should not replace competent medical and/or psychological care. The authors and publishers are in no way liable for any use or misuse of the information.

Printed in the United States of America

1 2 3 4 5 6 7 8 9 04 03 02 01 00

THROW LIKE A
Girl

Discovering the Body, Mind, and Spirit of the Athlete in You!
by Shelley Frost and Ann Troussieux

Gareth Stevens Publishing
A WORLD ALMANAC EDUCATION GROUP COMPANY

About the Authors

Daily workouts on her Stairmaster, healthy eating, and power walks with her dog, Keethy, keep Shelley Frost feeling strong and energetic. Shelley uses lots of energy playing sports with her six-year-old son, producing documentaries, and writing screenplays.

Ann Troussieux got her start in sports through an after-school rec program in elementary school. By high school, Ann played three to four competitive sports a year. Ann enjoys running, soccer, and playing sports with her two children, Claire and Remy. She is currently the vice president of TRAC, a company specializing in software solutions for nonprofit organizations.

Acknowledgments

To everyone who shared our belief that this book needed to be created in an age where sports opportunities for girls have never been more available, beneficial, and life-changing. We would like to thank our families, Kevin and Bret and Christian, Claire, and Remy; our editors, Michelle Roehm and Barbara Mann; our agents, Shelley Lewis and Seth Robertson; our parents, Nancy Ruff and Michael and Dolores O'Brien; our mentors, Anne Cribbs and Joanie Greggains; Ann's teammates, Ellen Barton, Maria Benech, and Katherine Kielty; and the many friends, relatives, girls, and women who generously gave us their feedback and support—Maureen Carroll, Donna O'Brien, Chris O'Brien, Dana Levy, Connie Beal, Katrin Tobin, Valerie Miller, and Ann's nieces. But most of all, we honor and thank the many girls and women who took the time to share their courageous stories with us.

Additional Editing Thanks
Laura Biermaier, Laura Carlsmith, Erin Doty, Mary Lou Kunold, and Mya Robertson.

Photography Thanks
Our super-buff girl models, Sara Arnold, Erin Doty, Samantha Ewers, Charlotte Roehm, and Ashlee Shelton, and our photographer, Jeff Van Raden.

Table of Contents

Introduction   6

Chapter 1   Why Throw Like a Girl?   9

Chapter 2   Individual Sports versus Team Sports:
Discover the Sport That's Right for You!   17

Chapter 3   Body:
Nutrition for the Athlete, Not the Super Model   37

Chapter 4   Body:
Year-Round Fitness   55

Chapter 5   Mind:
Relaxation, Goal Setting, Imagery, and Self-Talk   73

Chapter 6   Spirit:
Staying Up When Others Are Getting You Down   87

Chapter 7   Scholarships and Careers for the
Sports-Savvy Girl   107

Chapter 8   This Could Be You! Real Women Talk about
How Sports Changed Their Lives   123

Sports Resources   145

Sources   153

Glossary   157

Index   158

Introduction

When we were young, playing sports helped us get through tough times and taught us life lessons. Sports turned our lives around, allowing us to gain self-confidence and to form positive relationships with those around us.

Shelley's Story

 In junior high school, I always wore my red corduroy coat, even on the hottest days. I was so ashamed of myself and my body that I never wanted to take that coat off. I was totally withdrawn. No friends, no confidence, no life. Then it all changed. How? I joined the church softball team. Suddenly, it was as if I had crossed into a new world filled with friends and fun. My body became fit. My energy and grades improved. Pretty soon, the red corduroy coat was forgotten, collecting dust bunnies on my closet floor.

Ann's Story

 My teammates from school might say my most memorable sports experience was the time I nailed a basket in a game against our arch rival, just as the buzzer sounded. But really, my fondest memories aren't about glory—they are of my dad sitting in the stands, supporting me; my teammates and I wrapping our shins and French braiding each other's hair before a game; the long bus rides after a disappointing loss; the killer laps we ran to pay penance. More than anything, sports have given me lasting friendships, the strength to stand up for what I believe in, and the character to keep trying when everyone else says it's all over.

HERE'S WHY IT'S SO COOL TO THROW LIKE A GIRL: The roots of

Looking back, we can see how our experiences in sports made us better people. We know how to take criticism and make it work for us. We know how to be positive role models and how to be "team players." We take care of our bodies by eating healthy foods, exercising regularly, and not using drugs or smoking cigarettes.

Sports Does a Girl Good

After all, what brings best friends and fun times together better than playing sports? You and your friends are all outside, passing the soccer ball, practicing a free throw, blocking a field hockey shot, laughing, joking, and having fun. But step back a moment and you might notice a few things. Maybe one girl has really improved her jump shot. Then there's another girl who's always helping everyone with tips and advice without making anyone feel dumb. And how could you ever win a game without the "motivator," your friend who keeps everyone energized and in high spirits? Self-confidence, support from friends, and staying out of trouble are just a few of the benefits that you'll get from sports.

Title IX

Luckily, even our country's leaders have recognized how beneficial sports are for girls. In 1972 they passed a law called Title IX that requires all public schools, including colleges and universities, to provide the same opportunities in sports for women and girls that they had already been providing for men and boys. For the first time in history, a young woman could win a basketball scholarship that would pay for school.

So why not get involved in sports? Because of Title IX, the future for girls in sports is now wide open. Whether you're interested in becoming a doctor in sports medicine, planning to be a point guard in the WNBA, or if you just want to have fun, sports can be a positive part of your life throughout school and well into your future.

modern baseball come from a game played exclusively by women in

Body, Mind, and Spirit!

Even if you've never set foot on a basketball court, or ridden a snowboard down a mountainside, or caught a wave on a surfboard, this book will inspire you to get involved in a sport that suits you. For those of you who already love sports but want to know how to eat for your best performance, what exercises to do to stay in shape, or how to avoid landing on the bench with an injury, look no further. Plus, we've included tips on how to handle common sports dilemmas like name-calling boys, angry teammates, and negative coaches. You'll discover how you can earn a sports scholarship for college, and you'll learn about exciting careers you can have in sports. There are even sports quizzes and activities to help you determine your athletic style. *Throw Like a Girl* reveals all the benefits, challenges, and possibilities sports can open up in your life and how to get the most out of what sports have to offer.

But just don't take it from us. Take it from the many girls who helped us write *Throw Like a Girl*! Their horror stories and their triumphant victories will make you cringe and cheer. Their advice on how to eat right, stay fit, and keep positive while playing sports will motivate you to make the most out of any sports situation. Most of all, their stories show how "throwing like a girl" is no longer an insult but a compliment they are proud to have earned!

medieval England called <u>stoolball</u>. ☼ Women's water polo was first

8

Chapter 1

Why Throw Like a Girl?

Quiz

Your sports profile—are you laid back or on the attack?

1. Your best friend's family has invited you to join them for a weekend at the lake on their houseboat. You:
   a) first find out if they have a ski boat; if you're going to be on the lake for an entire weekend there had better be some wake jumping in the plans!

   b) pack your bikini and suntan lotion; it's about time you get to work on your tan.
   c) tell them that sounds great and secretly hope that there are some good hiking trails around the lake.

2. It's your first day snowboarding and you have an extra hour before you head home. You decide to:
   a) try out that jump your instructor showed you.
   b) head straight for the lodge to get some hot chocolate.
   c) meet your buddies for one last run on the bunny slope.

3. You and a group of your friends decide to tackle the 4-hour hike to that well-known waterfall in the canyon. When your group starts out, you:
   a) lead the pack! You want to be the first to make it to the top and get your feet wet!
   b) mix in the middle. The point of this whole hike is to hang with your friends, right? And you know the moral support will keep you going!
   c) bring up the rear. Hey, what's the harm in taking your time? The waterfall's not going anywhere.

4. You're staying with your grandparents in Florida for the summer. The first thing you do when you arrive is:
   a) surf the 160 channels on the satellite TV.
   b) rent a bike and check out the sights around town.
   c) sign up for scuba diving lessons.

included in the Olympics in 2000, wiping out the last men-only team

5. You and your family are driving through a national park on your family vacation. You stop at a rest area and your mom gives you an hour of free time. You:
    a) find the nearest trail and see how far you can get. You don't want to let this great mountain go to waste.
    b) race your little sister around the bathroom. Your legs could really use some stretching after all that time in the car.
    c) seek out the nearest shady tree after begging a soda off your mom. It's hot!!

6. Your gym class is picking partners for badminton. You:
    a) immediately pick the buffest girl in the class. You want to win!
    b) grab anybody in the class and start serving. The point is to have fun!
    c) pick your closest buddy. Badminton just isn't your thing so might as well make the most of it.

7. You meet your best friend at the local ice rink for the afternoon session on Saturday. You:
    a) make it your goal to see how fast you can speed around the rink. So what if your friend can't keep up?
    b) hang with your friend and practice your figure eights.
    c) skate a couple of times around the rink and then convince your friend to visit the snack bar. Maybe you can talk to the cute guy at the counter!

Scoring

1. a- 3, b- 1, c- 2	5. a- 3, b- 2, c- 1
2. a- 3, b- 1, c- 2	6. a- 3, b- 2, c- 1
3. a- 3, b- 2, c- 1	7. a- 3, b- 2, c- 1
4. a- 1, b- 2, c- 3	

21–18 points. Thrill Seeker. You are a true explorer, always searching for the next adventure. Unfortunately, you're sometimes so adventuresome that you have a hard time waiting for others to catch up. Sports you might like: surfing, snowboarding, mountain biking, and climbing.

17–11 points. The Sporty Girl. Like the thrill seeker, you love sports and trying new things but you're also willing to take the extra time to help your friends learn too. Sports you might like: tennis, soccer, basketball, skiing, and swimming.

10–7 points. Maxing and Relaxing. Though you find sports interesting, you mainly view them as a good opportunity to hang out with friends. Sports you might like: pool, bowling, hiking, and water skiing.

sport in the games. ✪ Water polo originated in the rivers and lakes of

Did you know that playing sports can improve your self-confidence, make you proud of your body and its athletic abilities, teach you about being a leader, allow you to learn from others, and help you stay out of trouble? Sports can rock your world! Don't believe us? Check out what these girls have to say about how sports made a difference in their lives.

Boost Your Self-Confidence

Studies have shown that playing sports can increase your self-confidence. Why do you think that is? Besides using your body in sports, you're putting your brain to work too. Great athletes work hard to think positive about themselves and their sport.

Girls Rock!—and Rock Climb!

"Rock climbing is a special sport to us. Sometimes when you're climbing, there's one grip you just can't reach. Finally, you reach it and get to the top. You look down and you see the same grip, but it looks so much smaller. You think, how could I have thought that something that little could have stopped me? Learning to think like that gives you a lot of self-confidence, not just in rock climbing but in other things too."
—**Emily Goldberg, age 11, Anna Siegel, age 12, and Rachael Kutler, age 11, rock climbers**

Feel Good about Your Body

As you start playing sports, you might see your body develop a "specialty." Maybe you have a strong right arm, or perhaps you can kick the heck out of a soccer ball—with your left foot! When your body shows off its abilities, what's there to be ashamed of?

19th-century England as an aquatic version of rugby. ☉ Skiing began

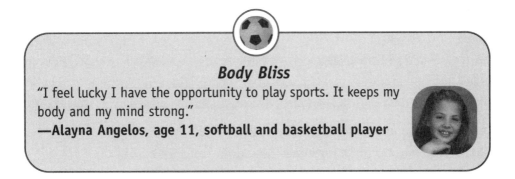

Body Bliss

"I feel lucky I have the opportunity to play sports. It keeps my body and my mind strong."
—**Alayna Angelos, age 11, softball and basketball player**

Strengthen Friendships

For any girl, playing sports can open up a world of new friendships. Being on a team gives you a built-in group of friends. Plus, while hanging out together, you'll really get to know each other. Besides the actual games there are practices, pizza meetings, bus rides to games, and victory celebrations.

Best Buds

"I did not have a really good school year with friends, and swimming helped me with that. I had been really hurt, and I was having a rough time emotionally. Swimming helped me make new friends and raised my self-esteem so I could reach my goal."
—**Kelsey Blegen, age 12, swimmer**

"My most memorable soccer experience is when my very best friend (the one who brought me into soccer) scored a goal in our first game."
—**Kimberly Bowen, age 11, soccer player**

as a form of transportation for people living in the mountains of

Learn Life Skills

Playing sports can even help you get better grades. Studies show that high school girls who play sports have higher grades than nonathletic girls. Whether you're part of a team or playing an individual sport, you're learning how to discipline yourself. And because you're so busy, your time is precious. This makes you a better time manager. Since you know you only have one hour to finish that math assignment, there are no ifs, ands, or buts about it. The work gets done.

Gaining Knowledge

"Everyone should be involved in a sport because it teaches you many things like cooperation and loyalty, develops your social skills, relieves stress, and most of all gives you a feeling of well being."
—Melissa Sailor, age 12, ice-hockey player

"I always take school first, then sports. I'm in a lot of after-school activities—Girl Scouts, first chair clarinet, student council, D.A.R.E., Spanish club, and always have time to help my neighbors."
—Sharron Larkin, age 12, swimmer and basketball player

Lead the Way!

Most likely the first woman to be president will look back over her life and proudly tell the world that playing sports brought her to where she is today. She will be living proof of what one study has already shown—that 80% of women leaders remember themselves as "tomboys" who actively participated in sports in their childhood. Not only can you have a blast playing sports, you'll also learn how to be competitive, yet cooperative; how to take criticism; how to

Europe. Skis were a way to visit neighbors at lower elevations. ❍ In the

deal with success and failure; and how to control anger and stress. What better qualities would you want for the next world leader?

Taking Control

"Sports have improved my leadership. You've got to work with your team to do the best you can. Everyone has to be a leader on the court. Sometimes you have to stand up and be a part of the team."
—Kelly Ostrem, age 12, basketball player

Stay Out of Trouble

Teens face many difficult choices—drugs, drinking, sex, cigarettes—but many girl athletes have a better sense of responsibility. They know how to set goals and how to keep their priorities straight. Also, girl athletes have strong, healthy bodies. It would be pretty hard to sprint a 100-meter dash after puffing on a cigarette.

However, sometimes girls will be tempted to choose the wrong path and hang out with the wrong crowd. A better choice would be to join a team. Forming friendships with other girls who share your interests and finding a coach who inspires and challenges you will send you down the right path to a brighter future.

Positive Action

"Surfing makes me want to do good things for myself and not hurt my own body with drugs. I have never tried any type of drug and I don't plan on doing any because I don't want to damage my body. Instead of taking drugs, I surf."
—Tory Titcomb, age 14, surfer

tenth grade, Gwen Torrence set a state record in the 220-yard dash

These girls know that doing sports can be both uplifting and empowering. Their experiences and comments reveal how sports can give you more self-confidence, a positive body image, leadership abilities, and keep you on the right track. The life skills that you can learn from sports won't just help you today, they'll help you through college, future careers, and in new friendships. Like these girls, you can use sports to learn more about yourself and the world around you. So get involved in sports and discover the mind, body, and spirit of the athlete in you!

Throw Like a Girl!

"I guess it is okay to say that I 'Throw like a Girl!' The interesting thing about it is that I throw people! Am I awesome? Well, I've taken the gold several times nationally, and usually the State Championship in West Virginia. I was the U.S. Jujitsu Junior Team Captain at the world championships. Who says I'm not awesome? Let's just step outside!!!"
—**Alicia Hughes-Skandijs, age 14,**
   U.S. Jujitsu Junior Team Captain

while wearing low-heeled patent leather pumps! She later became an

Chapter 2

Individual Sports versus Team Sports: Discover the Sport That's Right for You!

Quiz

Are you the team type or a solo act?

1. Your class is sponsoring the spring dance and needs lots of volunteers. You're the first to sign up to:
   a) design the invitations on your computer.
   b) negotiate the contract with the deejay.
   c) join the cleanup crew.

2. A friend asks you and your friends over to temporarily dye your hair Kool-Aid red. You say:
   a) "Count me in!" If anyone decides to give you a hard time they'll have a group of angry redheads to deal with.
   b) "Forget it!" If you're going to dye your hair, you aren't about to share the attention with anyone!
   c) "Whatever." You aren't a huge fan of red but if they are really into it, what the heck?

3. You're struggling over today's math assignment, so you:
   a) try to organize a study group.
   b) spend the extra time to figure it out on your own.
   c) call a couple friends for help.

4. Your mom is begging you to join a club at school. You love to sing, so to get her off your back for a while, you sign up for:
   a) the school concert choir; hey you've got some talent but you're no Mariah Carey yet.
   b) private voice lessons; you've got some pipes and you aren't about to be drowned out by 20 sopranos!
   c) both; if your mom wants you to join a club you'll show her just how involved you can be!

5. You, some friends, and your family decide to go camping for the weekend. Upon arriving at the campsite, you:
   a) use your outdoor survival knowledge to get the fire going.
   b) help your little brothers set up the tent.
   c) join your friends in making marshmallow sticks for the campfire later—let's get our priorities straight here.

Olympic medalist in track and field. ✪ Before J.C. Babcock invented a

6. It's the first school dance of the year and you are so nervous you're out of finger-nails to chew. To calm your nerves you:
   a) call every single one of your friends to find out what she is wearing and her estimated arrival time.
   b) ask your best friend to hang out with you as much as possible (except for the slow dances of course).
   c) find the newest style the mall has to offer and rest assured that no one else will be wearing the same dress.

7. It's the Women's World Cup and all of your girlfriends are meeting to watch the game and cheer for their favorite team (they all have the same favorite team). Since your team didn't even make the semifinals you:
   a) cheer for the other team; if your gals take the trophy you'll have the satisfaction of winning and all of the glory to yourself.
   b) who cares? You're there for the chip and dip not the cheerleading!
   c) cheer for the same team; if they win you'll have a room full of friends to celebrate with.

Scoring

1. a- 1, b- 2, c- 3   5. a- 1, b- 2, c- 3
2. a- 3, b- 1, c- 2   6. a- 3, b- 2, c- 1
3. a- 3, b- 1, c- 2   7. a- 1, b- 2, c- 3
4. a- 3, b- 1, c- 2

21–18 points. Team Player. You love your buds and you like the energy and support that a group can generate. You may feel totally confident doing the job alone but it's a lot more fun to share the glory with your teammates. Suggested sports: soccer, basketball, volleyball, rowing, and hockey are sports that will allow you to shine.

17–11 points. Team or Individual Player. Though you enjoy hanging out in a group, you also value your independence. Suggested sports: swimming, track, skiing, and bowling are sports that have both individual and team competitions.

10–7 points. Individual Player. Team sports are fine but nothing beats the feeling of having all eyes, as well as all responsibility, on you. You like to be the best at what you can do. You not only challenge your competitors, you also constantly challenge yourself to do better. Suggested sports: diving, cross-country running, billiards, gymnastics, golf, and martial arts are sports that will allow the competitor in you to thrive.

rolling seat in 1857, rowers greased their pants or used oatmeal to help

Just as every girl has her own unique style that expresses something about herself, the same is true for sports. Whether you prefer team sports, individual sports, or like to participate in both, there is a sport out there for you. For girls who don't already have a sport they love or who want to try something new, this chapter will help you get on the team or in the action fast!

Me, Myself, and I:
Sports for the Independent Girl

Girls who like to manage their own time and who like to set their own goals may prefer to choose an individual sport geared toward personal achievement. In most individual sports, you will need to find a coach or take lessons to improve your technique and develop a training program. Many individual sports also have team opportunities that give you the option to compete on your own or with a team.

To make doubly sure you're an individual-sports kind of gal ask yourself these questions: Can you be your own cheerleader? Has it always been easy for you to talk yourself into exercising? Is there a personal trainer inside your head who tells you when to pick up the pace and move faster? If so, one or more of the sports described on the next few pages just might grab you. Who knows, maybe there's a rock climber or surfer in you just waiting to be let loose!

them slide in the boat. ✪ Before the 1700s, ballerinas danced in long

Pros and Cons of Solo Sports

Archery

Pros—Bull's eye!

Cons—Difficult to practice if you live in an apartment.

Bicycling

Pros—Great workout, beautiful scenery, and good way to explore.

Cons—Lots of safety equipment—be sure to wear a helmet!

Billiards (Pool)

Pros—Good for math, geometry, physics, and very social.

Cons—Make sure there's a handy pool table.

Bowling

Pros—Groovy shoes!

Cons—Gutter balls!

Canoeing/Kayaking

Pros—Lots of wildlife!

Cons—Heavy boats that you need help carrying.

Climbing

Pros—Incredible views!

Cons—Lots of gear, training, and adult supervision.

Cross-Country Skiing

Pros—Peaceful, great aerobic workout, and usually free.

Cons—Watch out for those hills!

Dancing

Pros—You'll never feel awkward at school dances.

Cons—*Pointe* shoes!

dresses, corsets, and slippers with heels! ✿ In 1987, Steffi Graf became

Diving

Pros—Adrenaline rushes.
Cons—Belly flops.

Downhill Skiing

Pros—Speed.
Cons—Speed.

Equestrian/Horseback Riding

Pros—If you love animals, you'll be in heaven!
Cons—Have you ever shoveled horse manure?

Fencing

Pros—How cool would you look with that *sword* in your hand?
Cons—Ouch!!!

Golf

Pros—Great pro sport for women—you can earn big bucks.
Cons—Those plaid knickers are expensive!

Gymnastics

Pros—One of the few sports you can do to music!
Cons—Cartwheels on a 4-inch-wide beam.

Hiking

Pros—GORP!
Cons—Switchbacks.

Ice Skating

Pros—Lots of pro opportunities.
Cons—Ever fallen on the ice in tights?

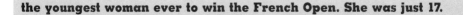

the youngest woman ever to win the French Open. She was just 17.

In-Line Skating

Pros—Good way to get around.

Cons—Hard to stop—can you say road rash?!

The Martial Arts:
Aikido, Judo, Tae Kwon Do/Karate

Pros—Great for learning self-defense.

Cons—If you're a pacifist, these may not be the sports for you.

The Martial Arts (Western Variations):
Kickboxing, Tae Bo

Pros—Very aerobic.

Cons—Let's just say . . . be sure to stretch.

Racquetball/Squash/Tennis

Pros—Wicked serves!

Cons—Balls that go straight for your face.

Running

Pros—You can do it almost anywhere at anytime.

Cons—Dogs, cars, and rain.

Snowboarding

Pros—This is not your parents' sport!

Cons—Ever heard of the slingshot fall?

Swimming

Pros—A total body workout!

Cons—Green hair. Yikes!

○ **The first Olympics were held in 776 B.C. and consisted of a**

Surfing

Pros—Sunshine, fresh air, nice tan.
Cons—Sharks!

T'ai Chi

Pros—Increased agility, flexibility, and improved posture.
Cons—Hyper? Pick another sport.

Track and Field Sports

Pros—Legs like Jackie Joyner-Kersey.
Cons—Watch out for flying javelins!

Water Skiing

Pros—Wake jumping!
Cons—Need a boat and lots of sunscreen.

Windsurfing

Pros—Great upper-body workout.
Cons—Windburn *and* sunburn.

Wrestling

Pros—Learn to headlock your big brother.
Cons—Body slams!

Yoga

Pros—Relaxing—a stress buster!
Cons—Wacky poses.

Check out the Sports Resources Guide on page 145 for more information on these sports.

200-meter dash. The all-male athletes ran in the nude and women who

Solo Sports

"Don't say you can't do it until you try. I was not going to play track and field because I thought I would not be good at it. If I would have listened to the other kids telling me that I was not strong enough or good enough, I would not have been successful. I used their words to motivate me to prove them wrong."

—Gretchen Chomas, age 15, basketball player and discus thrower

 "I considered dropping tennis for basketball or something that all my friends did. Looking back, I am glad and proud that I stuck to my sport and it has paid off."

—Jennifer Schwenk, age 13, tennis player

"My being deaf and blind makes other people amazed at my ability to ride a horse on my own. I think anyone with the will and determination can do it no matter what."

—Jennifer Hawkins, age 13, horseback rider

"There is one very memorable and cherished dance moment in my life so far. I could feel the energy start to build as we changed into our dance costumes. It grew when we entered backstage to await the end of the act

 before us. Then the energy level shot up as the music started. If you have ever gone skydiving, I would expect that you know the feeling that I had for the next four minutes: perfect and unending freedom, excitement."

—Victoria Sandbrook, age 14, dancer

Teaming Up

Playing team sports can be just as gratifying as playing individual sports. The difference is in the approach. In individual sports, you depend only on yourself to get the results you want. In team sports you

tried to watch were thrown off a cliff to their deaths! ☺ Babe Didrikson

must also depend on others to work hard. Team sports can bring as many challenges as rewards, but in the end, it's worth it and everyone benefits—especially you!

Being on a team does not always mean good times. Just as you share in the team's victory, you also share in its losses. Whatever the result, working with your teammates to win a game can be exhilarating, help to create new friendships, and improve your skills as a player.

Give It a Try!

"No matter what you do or how bad you might think you are, you should always try your best, because no one is born knowing how to play a sport. We all have to learn just like everyone else."
—Destri Dickey, age 9, soccer and baseball player

"When I first started the sixth grade I heard that my new school was lucky enough to have a swim and dive team. I just knew that was what I wanted to join. The first day of practice, our coach told the dive team (which I joined) to go outside and do stretches. When one of the eighth graders asked who hadn't been on a dive team before, nobody raised his or her hand. I didn't raise my hand either, even though I had never been on a dive team before. I was too embarrassed to admit I was the only one. When we were done with stretches, we went to the pool area, and everybody lined up for dives. When it was my turn, I got up and did my awkward version of the flip. When I was finished, I felt really embarrassed, but there was someone there to help me. An eighth grader was standing by the edge of the pool.

She told me that I wasn't ready for flips and stunts yet. For the next few days, I worked on a three steps and hurtle dive. I learned that it doesn't matter if you're the only one trying something new, or that you can't do this thing like a pro; it just matters that you can do it, and want to learn."
—Jessica Beck, age 11, diver

was such an all-around superstar athlete, when she competed in the

"When I first tried water polo I told my parents 'It's too hard!' I guarantee any girl who tries water polo as a new sport will feel the same way. I would advise you not to quit because when I first started it, I hated it. But now I understand the game and I am in much better shape. Stick with it, learn the rules, and give anything new a chance before giving up on it. If it is a sport, a teacher, or a new school subject, too many girls give up on new things in life before they really understand them. Hang in there and really give it a good try first."
—**Darby Anderson, age 11, water polo player**

"If you try out for a team and you are cut, don't stop playing because one person may not be able to see your talent and another may think that you have a lot of talent and they are willing to help you! Keep playing no matter what. Just remember Michael Jordan didn't make the cut when he first tried out for basketball and look at him now!!!"
—**Nicole Norton, age 13, basketball player**

"Once you have discovered the sport you love, be it bowling or softball, stay with it. I began bowling a year and a half ago with an average of 44 and a high game of 84. Now my average is 113, with my all time high at 172."
—**Julienne MillerLapp, age 13, bowler**

"The advice I have for other female athletes is never give up!"
—**Sara Rodriguez, age 11, basketball player**

Pre-Tryout Jitters

So . . . you've never played soccer before. Okay, you've played once, only that was two years ago! You're excited to join the school team but you're also nervous because you are completely clueless about the game. What do you do?

Even though being part of a team can be a great experience, it can also be intimidating, especially if it's your first time. Just realize that it's all right to feel nervous. It might help you to think of all the people out there who have participated in sports. They all had to go through what you're going through now *and they survived*, believe it or not! Besides, you have nothing to lose by trying.

There are many sports programs offered through local parks and recreation districts, religious groups like the YWCA, and schools. Often, these programs are the first exposure kids have to team sports. Many Olympic champions never even touched a ball before high school. So go for it—this may be the break you need before you move on to Olympic glory!

Now that you know you're not alone, the next step is to talk to the coach before the tryout. Find out what will be expected—the more prepared you are, the more confident you'll be. After getting the details from the coach, practice what you need to do with a friend. This will help you feel more relaxed when the big day comes.

enough points by herself to win the <u>team</u> title. ✪ In 1949, Babe founded

Greatness Isn't a Birthright

"Great athletes aren't born great, they have to work too. They aren't any more special than you. They just wanted something, tried, and succeeded."
—**Cassie Kipper, age 14, triathlete and runner**

Dream Team

You did it! You survived tryouts and you're on one of the best teams in the district. The practices are great but the coach is insane (she made the whole team run 20 laps last week). The girls on your team are cool, and everyone has helped you feel right at home. You're having a blast, but because you're new, you still haven't seen any action since you've joined the team. What's up?

Don't stress. Though your coach obviously appreciates your ability (you did make the team, after all!), she may be giving you some time to adjust to your new surroundings. Even if you are not in the game, use this time to take positive action. (This doesn't mean picking dandelions while your teammates are at the other end of the field!) Training or stretching while you're waiting to play are just a few of the things you can do to keep yourself focused.

Even from the sidelines you can still contribute tons to your team. Cheering and positive suggestions have helped more teams to succeed than anything else. Contributing to a team does not just mean playing, it means supporting the other players, on and off the field. After all, your team is the best because positive people like you are part of it!

the Ladies' Professional Golf Association. ✪ In 1951, Babe was asked if

Nightmare Team

So you didn't get on the dream team and the only team left hasn't won a game in four years. Do you decide to give up on your dreams of being the next Sheryl Swoopes? No way! This team has just been waiting for you to arrive. Your team spirit and enthusiasm might give your team the extra boost it needs to win. Best of all, your teammates have got guts and determination (especially after so many losses!) and they are willing to work hard to do well. Take a risk and put your best team skills to the test. Besides, everyone loves the underdog!

What Can I Bring to a Team?

If you've never been on a team before, you may be unaware of your personal team-player qualities. Without any experience, you might feel you don't have much to offer your team. But being a team player is a lot more than making a basket or scoring a goal. Enthusiasm, willingness to learn, and good attendance are just a few of the personal qualities that would be valued on any team.

Here are some examples of team qualities:
"I try to make sure that everyone is psyched before games."
"I'm funny so I try to come up with jokes to keep the team up."

You can write down your team qualities here:

_____

_____

_____

_____

_____

A positive attitude can make or break a team. With all the great team qualities you have, how could any team survive without you?

there was anything she **didn't** play. She replied, "Yeah, dolls." ✪ In 1927,

30

Pros and Cons of Team Sports

Baseball/Softball

Pros—One swing and it's outta here!
Cons—Killer curve balls.

Basketball

Pros—Three pointers!
Cons—Standing on the free-throw line can be lonely.

Football

Pros—Dancing in the end zone is a blast!
Cons—You can end up at the bottom of a dog pile.

Hockey

Pros—Good way to get your aggression out.
Cons—There's a *reason* why hockey players don't smile.

Lacrosse

Pros—One of the fastest moving games on two feet.
Cons—Watch out for flying objects!

Rugby

Pros—Find out where "touchdowns" really came from.
Cons—Mud galore!

Soccer

Pros—Be a part of the world's most popular sport.
Cons—Don't forget your shin guards!

Volleyball

Pros—Setting up your friend for the kill.
Cons—Net serves!

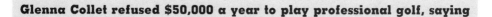

Glenna Collet refused $50,000 a year to play professional golf, saying

Water Polo

Pros—Combines the best of swimming, basketball, and soccer.

Cons—Be prepared to rip up a swim suit or two.

Teamwork

"Most people see the person who scored, as the one who won the game. But this isn't true. The whole team had to work hard for it, not just one person. When Brandy Chastain scored the winning goal in the shoot out of the Women's World Cup, she didn't do it by herself. Brianna Scurry had to make the save. Kristine Lilly had to head the ball off the goal line. *Everyone* has to be giving their best, 110% effort at all times. This is one of the hardest parts of the game."

—Jennifer Layton, age 13, soccer player

"Teamwork goes a long way in the equestrian world. We have to have teamwork with our horses, we each have to give and take, if one of us just takes and doesn't give, everything can go wrong."

—Meghan Sederholm, age 15, horseback rider

"I like team skating so that all the skaters are highlighted instead of having one 'star skater.' I love the teamwork involved and the friendships that I have made from the experience. I am even looking forward to skating on a college team one day."

—Kelly Dwyer, age 13, team ice-skater

"Playing on a team means not being a ball hog and not letting the other team members play by themselves. I learned the saying, 'work together, achieve more' from my choir leader. I think this is true in soccer also."

—Megan Johnson, age 7, soccer player

she played for pleasure, not for money. ✪ At the 1972 Olympics, Russian

"My team, Rage, probably has the hardest time any other team has to go through. We have been defeated many, many times, but we always keep our courage and spirit alive. My most memorable time was when we were scrimmaging and we were losing by eight points. I accidentally made a fool out of myself and scored a goal for the other team! I felt like crying but luckily my teammates were nice enough to let go of this whole incident."
—Arum Sukmawanto, age 11, soccer player

"In the sixth grade I tried out for basketball. Even though I didn't make it I decided to play in the city league. By the end of the season, I was selected to be on the All-Star Team. My advice is just because you didn't make the school team doesn't mean you can't play."
—Lauren Dumas, age 13, basketball player

"I always try to boost up the morale of my team by being positive and setting a good example."
—Kelly Werner, age 11, softball catcher

"Bowling is very team oriented. There is no pressure or emphasis on any one individual for having a lower score than would be ideal. Teammates just want each other to do their personal best and applaud each other for doing so. If you have a bad day, it's understood."
—Julienne MillerLapp, age 13, bowler

Start Your Own Team

If you can't find a team to play on, you can try starting your own team. Let's say you want to start a basketball team:

1. Decide where you'll play. Is there a city-owned park with basketball courts you can use? Do you have a basketball hoop in your driveway?

gymnast Olga Korbut became the first and only woman to do a back-

2. Get the word out. Make up flyers listing the location, date, and time of your first practice/game. Pass them along to friends who might be interested. Urge them to spread the word too. If you can, try to get enough people to form two teams so that you can eventually play each other.

3. Before your first game, get familiar with some warm-up exercises and practice drills. When you're able to lead the group with a serious workout, they'll have confidence that this game is not a one time event.

4. When everyone arrives, put on your take-charge attitude and get the practice going.

5. If everyone had fun, got a good workout, and made new friends, they will come again.

6. Don't forget to think up a cool name for your team!

Tracking Down Hard-to-Find Sports

What if you wanted to try fencing, or maybe those giant ocean breakers are calling to you? It's doubtful your school offers these sports. But the gung-ho girl is going to track down her sport-of-choice, no matter if she lives in a Manhattan apartment or in the mountains of Montana.

The best place to find a sports team that's right for you, besides your school, is your local recreation department or community center. These organizations are listed in the Yellow Pages and are usually run by your city government. Ask them to mail you a brochure or program guide listing all the classes, events, and programs they offer. Activities sponsored by cities and recreation districts are usually very affordable.

flip on the balance beam. ✪ In 1965, at the Bonneville Salt Flats in

If your city does not have a recreation department, try a church or other religious community center. Contact the activity director to see what kinds of sports programs they have. Also look in the Sports Resource Guide on page 145 for contact information on sports programs in your area.

Sports Camps

One good way to improve your ability and skills as an athlete is through a sports camp—you don't have to be an expert in a sport to attend! Many camps have all levels of instruction and competition. Most are held during the summertime and run from one week to several months. Some camps are day camps, and some are overnight camps. You will find camps that specialize in one sport, and others that offer sports galore.

Sports camps can be expensive, but local recreation departments, non-profit groups, or religious groups such as the YWCA, Campfire Girls, and Girl Scouts offer less expensive camps. Camp costs can range from $10 to $50 a day for day camps and $100 or more a day for residential camps. Many camps will provide you with sports equipment. In some cases you will be responsible for your personal gear (shin guards, knee pads, helmet, etc.) but the camp provides the rest. Call first to see what you need to bring.

What if you want to go with a friend? Often, camps will allow you to specify one buddy that you would like to be with. However, there are other camps that don't let you do this. These may be better camps for you if you're going by yourself. Then you won't have to worry about everyone being paired up when you arrive!

If you love to play sports but you don't like fierce competition, there are also camps that focus more on training and less on opponents. By asking the camp what its "mission statement" is, you can make sure the balance of competition is right for you.

Utah, Margaret "Lee" Breedlove set a women's land speed record, rac-

Camps and Organizations to Contact
for More Information

American Camping Association

(800) 777-CAMP

www.aca-ny.org

Camp Fire Boys and Girls

(816) 756-1950

www.campfire.org

CampPage Guide to Summer Camps

www.camppage.com

e-mail: webmaster@camppage.com

Girl Scouts Sports+

420 5th Ave.

New York, NY 10018

(800) 478-7248

www.gsusa.org

YWCA National Office

(800) 992-2871

www.ymca.net

ing at **308.65 miles per hour.** ✪ **Annie Taylor rode a barrel over**

Chapter 3

Body: Nutrition for the Athlete, Not the Super Model

Quiz

Are you a health nut or a doughnut?

1. You just got home from school and you're starving. You have:
   a) a bagel, some grapes, and a glass of milk.
   b) some crackers with cheese and a soda.
   c) a handful of chocolate chip cookies and a couple of cheese puffs.

2. You're making a smoothie before you head off to practice. Typically you make your smoothies with:
   a) yogurt and a banana.
   b) frozen yogurt, chocolate syrup, and some fresh fruit.
   c) chocolate ice cream and a candy bar, maybe a couple of cookies.

3. Your friends are discussing the latest fad diet. The next day you:
   a) run to the store to buy the book—you want all the details.
   b) skip breakfast.
   c) invite your friends over for dinner—pasta is your mom's specialty!

4. Some kids you play baseball with in the neighborhood offer you a cigarette. You:
   a) try it—hey, they're great at sports and it hasn't hurt them!
   b) pretend to smoke it—you don't want to get a hard time.
   c) tell them thanks but you'd rather have a smoothie.

5. After your triumphant victory over your arch rivals, your team decides to go out for pizza to celebrate. You make sure to:
   a) drink at least two 8-ounce glasses of water.
   b) have some water but also have a jumbo root beer.
   c) drink a jumbo root beer and a jumbo cola.

6. You've just started off your day with a 25-mile bike ride. You're pumped! You celebrate your accomplishment with:
   a) a hot fudge sundae—after all, you just rode 25 miles!
   b) a 1/2 pound burger—time to replenish all that protein you burned.
   c) two 8-ounce glasses of water and a plate of pasta—your body's talking to you.

7. You wake up late at night and your stomach is growling for a midnight snack. You sneak to the kitchen for:
   a) a half a turkey sandwich; it tastes good and won't give you a huge sugar rush before trying to sleep again.
   b) a couple of Ding Dongs—you haven't had your daily chocolate intake yet.
   c) a meatball sandwich followed by ice cream and leftover cheesecake—hey, what the stomach wants, the stomach gets.

Scoring

1. a- 1, b- 2, c- 3
2. a- 1, b- 2, c- 3
3. a- 3, b- 2, c- 1
4. a- 3, b- 2, c- 1
5. a- 1, b- 2, c- 3
6. a- 3, b- 2, c- 1
7. a- 1, b- 2, c- 3

21–18 points. Anything goes! You may be the local burger joint's favorite customer but I wouldn't brag just yet. Participating in sports requires added energy and stamina from your body—the milkshakes and cheeseburgers just aren't going to cut it. Mix in some pasta and fruit and we promise your arteries will thank you later.

17–11 points. Pretty good. You enjoy a healthy meal but tend to gravitate to the junk food when you're in a hurry. Tip: Think of your body like you would a car—when you give it bad gasoline it'll choke and spit, maybe even quit! When you give it premium gasoline, it'll run like a charm. Take the time to make yourself a hearty meal and you'll be charged all day long.

10–7 points. Super healthy! Good for you—you are aware of your health and tend to stick with a healthy diet. Your athletic performance will reflect that, but be cautious not to fall victim to silly fad diets. You are the most knowledgeable about your body and the foods that you put into it, so keep it up!

a professional basketball player, set a new record in 1993 for the most

Did you know that you need more nutrients and calories right now than at any other time in your life? Believe it or not, your body mass almost doubles during your teen years. (This doesn't mean your weight will double. Body mass is your body's entire contents: blood, bones, organs, skin—everything.) Sound like a nightmare? Well it's not. It's normal. Your body is growing so fast that it is more important now than ever to eat well. And if you're working out, you will need food to both energize you and help your body grow to its full potential.

The Food Pyramid

Okay, we know . . . you've seen it all before but take one more look at it from the viewpoint of an athlete. The Food Guide Pyramid of daily dietary recommendations is a great way to put the food servings you need as an athlete into perspective. The pyramid corresponds with the suggested amount of servings you should have from each food group. Foods found near the top of the pyramid, like fats and sugars, should be eaten only occasionally. Near or at the bottom of the pyramid are foods high in nutrients, such as complex carbohydrates (found in breads and cereals), fibers (found in vegetables and fruits), calcium (found in milk products and some vegetables), and protein (found in meat and beans). These foods should be eaten more often.

Though the food pyramid is a great guide for eating healthy, athletes may need more servings of food from different parts of the pyramid than nonathletes. How do you know which foods will benefit you the most? Here are some suggestions that will both optimize your performance as an athlete and energize your body.

Complex Carbs: Fuel for Your Body

For athletic girls, complex carbohydrates, such as breads, grains, pasta, fruit, and vegetables (located at or near the bottom of the pyramid), are your best sources of energy. When you eat a baked potato, the carbohydrates are broken down into glucose molecules—body fuel. These molecules flow through your bloodstream to energize and feed your brain, organs, and muscles. Some glucose is turned into a high energy source called glycogen which is the "energy drink" for your muscles. Glycogen helps your muscles to work harder and longer. So fill 'er up—with carbohydrates!

So now you're thinking, "If carbohydrates are so great, I guess I can get away with eating cookies and cake!" If only this were true. There are two kinds of carbohydrates: simple and complex. Simple carbohydrates, such as refined sugars and corn syrup, are found in your favorite desserts and provide you with empty calories. Complex carbohydrates, also known as starches and fibers, are in foods such as whole grain breads, cereals, pastas, potatoes, corn, rice, fruits, fruit juices, vegetables, and beans. These foods will fuel up your body for any workout, game, or practice.

Sixty percent of your daily calories should come from complex carbohydrates. The best time to supply your muscles with these carbohydrates is the first two hours *after* exercise because this is the peak time your body produces glycogen. Here are some great "after workout" snacks to keep your muscles going strong:

- Two pieces of fruit, such as bananas, oranges, or apples.
- Fruit juices such as cranberry, grapefruit, or orange.
- A cup of yogurt topped with blueberries or raspberries.
- A bagel and a cup of grapes.
- A bowl of cereal with skim milk and a sliced banana.
- A bran, cranberry, or blueberry muffin.

○ **Wilma Rudolph, dubbed the "fastest woman in the world" and the**

Fiber Cleans Up

Eating carbohydrates high in fiber is the best way to feel great and work at your peak performance. Fruits and vegetables are loaded with fiber and are a good source of vitamins. Fiber, also found in grains like bran, is not easily digested or absorbed by the body. This means when you eat foods rich in fiber your stomach will feel full and satisfied. Once the fiber has gone through your stomach, it travels through your digestive tract, scrubbing and cleaning along the way. Not eating enough fiber can cause you to feel sluggish and bloated. The following are some single-serving, fiber-rich foods:

Grains
(The Pyramid recommends 6 to 11 servings each day.)
> 1/2 cup bran cereal
> 1 bran waffle
> 1/2 cup oatmeal
> 1 slice whole wheat bread
> 1 small bran muffin

Vegetables
(The Pyramid recommends 3 to 5 servings each day.)
> 1 cup of spinach (or other leafy vegetable)
> 1/2 cup raw carrots
> 1/2 cup cooked broccoli
> 1/2 cup cooked corn

Fruits
(The Pyramid recommends 2 to 4 servings each day.)
> 1 medium-sized apple, banana, or orange
> 1/4 cup raisins
> 1/2 cup cooked or canned fruit

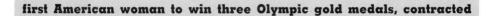
first American woman to win three Olympic gold medals, contracted

Snack Attack

For many girls, their favorite meal of the day is not breakfast, lunch, or dinner—it's snack time! In fact, research shows that girls get 30% of their daily nutrition needs from snack foods. Though snacking should never replace regular meals, it can offer an important source of nutrition. If you're going to snack (and we know you are) you might as well try out some healthy snacks.

 Here are some yummy "grab-n-go" foods that are healthier than cookies, chips, or ice cream:

Bagels, pretzels, animal crackers, cereal bars, chocolate-covered peanuts, yogurt, mozzarella sticks, air-popped popcorn, rice cakes, bananas, apples, pears, and grapes.

Bone Up on Foods Rich in Calcium

During your teens, your bones are developing at warp speed. Your skeleton might seem permanent, but the bone in it is constantly being formed and reabsorbed back into your body. When your skeleton is 12 years old, it is only half grown and will double in size by the time you are an adult. Calcium is the mineral that makes your teeth and bones grow strong and healthy. Many foods in the pyramid, like milk, cheese, yogurt, broccoli, and spinach, contain calcium.

Of course, it seems like the distant future, but by the time you reach 35, your body will begin losing bone mass. Extreme bone loss is a condition called osteoporosis. Women with osteoporosis have weak, brittle bones that can break with everyday movements (like turning a doorknob!). If you want to be active and play sports as an adult too, fragile bones will not get you back to home plate. Now is the time to bone up on your calcium!

polio when she was four and was told that she would never walk again.

Research indicates that girls need at least 1300 mg of calcium daily. According to the Food Pyramid that would be about 2 to 3 servings of calcium-rich foods each day.

Calcium-rich Foods

cup of plain yogurt	450 mg
cup of milk	301 mg
cup of calcium-fortified orange juice	300 mg
3 oz Swiss cheese (3 slices)	816 mg
cup of spinach	244 mg
cup of broccoli	70 mg
cup of collard greens	230 mg
1 oz almonds (25 almonds)	75 mg

The Champion Calcium Breakfast

When you first wake up in the morning, calcium is probably the last thing on your mind. But breakfast foods are some of the best sources for calcium. Studies show that teen girls are more likely to skip breakfast, eat fewer meals at home, and avoid drinking milk. And on average, girls only take in half of their recommended daily amount of calcium. A glass of milk furnishes 30% of your daily calcium requirement, and a cup of yogurt is another 30%. Together they contribute 60% of the 130% daily goal for calcium. If this was your breakfast, you would be halfway to fulfilling your daily calcium requirement at only eight o'clock in the morning!

Take just 10 minutes each morning to down some breakfast, and great things will happen:

- You'll be more alert in school, which will help you ace that pop quiz.
- You'll be energized, ready to jump into class and sports activities.

○ **Women didn't start wearing shorts in tennis until 1931 when Lili de**

Afternoon Snacks for Strong Bones

For afternoons when your stomach's growling so loudly that you can't hear yourself think, smoothies can satisfy your hunger *and* your calcium requirement.

Smoothie Shakes

Blend the following ingredients into a blender, using proportions of your own liking:

Crushed ice
Vanilla frozen yogurt
Cranberry juice or orange juice
Bananas with fresh or frozen fruit, such as strawberries, raspberries, or blueberries

Protein Pays Off

In the old days, moms would tell their kids, "If you want to put some meat on your bones, eat your meat!" This is because meat provides protein, the "building blocks" of our bodies.

Why is protein so important to a girl's growing body? When you eat a plate of scrambled eggs, your body breaks down the proteins into amino acids—think of these acids as the boards, nails, bricks, and cement of your body. In order to keep your body in good repair, you need to eat foods that can provide you with these amino acids. Protein can be found in many parts of your body: hair, skin, muscles, bones, blood, major organs, even in your hormones. If you were stuck on a desert island with only coconuts to eat, your body might start showing signs of protein loss—good-bye teeth and hair!

So how much protein do you need? Though some protein, like meat, eggs, milk, beans, and nuts, is essential to your health, a small amount of these foods will give you all the protein you need. A teenager needs 1 gram of protein for each 2.2 pounds of body weight. If you weigh 120 lbs., you will need about 54 grams each day (or 2-3 servings according to the Food Pyramid), which would be the equivalent of all of the following:

One breast of chicken or filet of fish (3 ounces)
One tall glass of milk (8 ounces)
One egg
That's it!!

Besides meat and dairy products, here are some other protein foods: peanut butter, nuts, lentils, tofu, calcium-fortified soy milk.

A Winning Pregame Meal

It's not only what you eat that affects athletic performance, it's when you eat. Here are some tips for planning pregame meals:

- Meals should be eaten 3 to 4 hours before the game.
- Meals should be high in carbohydrates, should have little protein and even less fat, and no more than 500 calories. For example, a turkey sandwich on two slices of bread, 1/2 cup corn, 8 ounces of milk, and one medium orange is a meal rich in nutrients and with the right proportions of carbohydrates, proteins, and fats.
- Avoid spicy, gas-producing, high fiber foods. (Now's not the time for a honkin' huge burrito!)
- Avoid sugary drinks within an hour of the game.
- Drink plenty of water before, during, and after the game.

ularized the Zamboni (that car that drives on the ice and smooths it out)

Chewin' the Fat

Is fat good for you? Believe it or not, there is good news about fat. Just as shin guards on the soccer field keep your shins from getting black and blue, fats protect your body in many ways: they insulate it from cold temperatures; they protect your organs and nerve pathways; they help some vitamins get absorbed into your body.

But there's also some bad news. Too much fat in your body contributes to many health hazards such as heart disease and cancer. That's why it's way at the top of the pyramid. It is recommended that you get no more than 30% (or about 1/3) of your daily calories from fat. This is where label reading comes in handy. When looking at the "Nutrition Facts" label, find the percentage of calories from fat. Compare it to the total number of calories per serving. If the fat-calorie percentage is high, this is a food you might want to skip. Here are two labels—one from a frozen chicken pot pie and one from a frozen chicken stir fry to help you make the comparison:

The Sugar Zap

Do you have a sweet tooth that harasses you for handouts? There is no doubt that cravings for a slice of pie or a glazed doughnut can over-power you from time to time. That's okay, as long as you eat your treats in moderation. Like fat, simple carbohydrates such as processed sugar are at the top of the food pyramid. Translation: Keep sugar to a mini-mum! A piece of candy or a bite of chocolate after a well-balanced meal should keep that sweet tooth happy.

by taking it with her around the world on skating tours. ○ Roberta

Say your stomach starts to growl, signaling it's time to fuel up your body. If you choose to eat a stack of chocolate chip cookies, you may feel satisfied for an hour or so, but soon after you'll be ready for a nap. This is because the energy burst you got from the sugar filtered through your blood stream, raced through your pancreas, morphed into insulin that steamrolled into your liver, which got overloaded, because its job is to get rid of the extra sugar. Phew! Now do you understand why you're so exhausted? To keep your body powered up instead of pooped out:

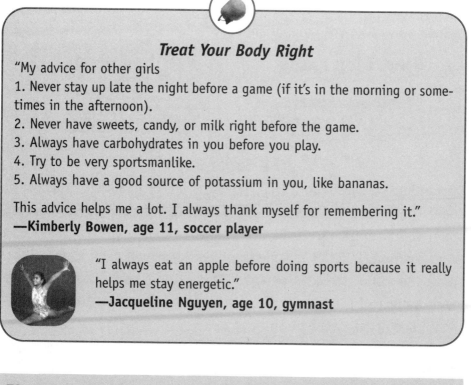

1. Go for sparkling water instead of soda pop.

2. Any food whose label reads "high fructose corn syrup," just put back on the shelf and slowly back away.

3. Switch to whole grain breads.

Treat Your Body Right

"My advice for other girls
1. Never stay up late the night before a game (if it's in the morning or sometimes in the afternoon).
2. Never have sweets, candy, or milk right before the game.
3. Always have carbohydrates in you before you play.
4. Try to be very sportsmanlike.
5. Always have a good source of potassium in you, like bananas.

This advice helps me a lot. I always thank myself for remembering it."
—**Kimberly Bowen, age 11, soccer player**

"I always eat an apple before doing sports because it really helps me stay energetic."
—**Jacqueline Nguyen, age 10, gymnast**

Bingay was the first woman to run the Boston Marathon in 1966. She

Water Your Body

Your body's skin, muscle, and bones appear solid. Yet 65% of your body is made up of water! Just through breathing and urinating, your body loses about 4% of its water content each day. Toss in your regular sports activities where sweating is the name of the game, and water becomes the star player on your team.

Drink at Least 8 Cups of Water Each Day

What does your body do with all that water?

- Water keeps your organs and digestive tract moist and lubricated so food and nutrients can easily be absorbed. Nutrients from food build strong bones and muscles which will improve your freestyle swim stroke.
- Water allows your brain to do its thinking. Clear thoughts and sharp observation will help you score goals.
- Water maintains your vision and lubricates your muscles. Hand-eye coordination will help you catch that fly ball.
- Water allows you to perspire (or sweat), keeping your body cool during strenuous exercises and flushing toxins out of your system. Endurance will get you across that finish line.

Test Your Hydration Expertise

Become a "hydration expert" by taking the following test and one day you may be able to help someone whose body is showing signs of water loss. Check which symptoms you think are signs of dehydration:

___ dizziness

___ breathing rapidly

___ dry eyes

___ nausea

___ flushed skin

___ complete exhaustion

___ cold and sweaty skin

___ cramping and spasming muscles

wore a hooded sweatshirt to hide her gender during the race! ۞ It wasn't

If you checked all eight symptoms, consider yourself a pro. Should you ever come across a person suffering from dehydration, call a doctor. The doctor will probably recommend drinking fluids, but if the person is suffering from severe dehydration, she may need to visit a hospital where she can receive fluids through an IV to speed up the rehydration process. An IV is an intravenous tube that goes directly into a vein. Ouch! Better to just keep that squirt bottle close!

Check Which Activities Help Prevent Dehydration:

1. __ splashing cool water over your head, face, and shoulders
2. __ drinking cup after cup of coffee or caffeinated tea
3. __ drinking soda and sugary drinks
4. __ drinking 8 cups or more of water each day
5. __ wearing loose-fitting, natural fiber clothing
6. __ working out during the coolest time of the day

All except #2 and #3 help to prevent dehydration. The caffeine in coffee, tea, and soda is a diuretic which causes you to urinate more which equals greater water loss. And the sugar in soda and other sweet drinks slows your body's absorption of liquids. If it's flavor you need, quench your thirst with sugar-free sports drinks. They contain minerals called electrolytes that help to balance the fluid levels in your body.

Ideal Hydration for Athletes

Sport Sequence	Amount of Water to Drink
2 hours before game/event	1-1 1/2 cups
10–15 minutes before game/event	1 1/4 cups
Every 15 minutes, during game/event	1/2 cup
After game/event	1-2 cups

until the 1920s that it was acceptable for women to wear pants or shorts

So carry that water bottle wherever you go, and your body will always be well watered.

Can an Athlete Go Vegetarian?

Food choices can make all the difference in how well highly active people perform in their sport or physical activity. A vegetarian diet can be a positive lifestyle choice, as long as you eat foods that provide your body with protein, iron, calcium, zinc, and vitamin B_{12}, all of which are necessary to remain healthy and active. Here are some food alternatives to meat that provide you with the same nutrients:

Protein—milk, cheese, beans, breads, cereals, nuts, peanut butter, tofu, and fortified soy milk.

Iron—dark, leafy green vegetables, iron-fortified cereals, apricots, bran flakes, and spinach.

Zinc—pumpkin seeds, eggs, mushrooms, soy beans, and nuts.

Vitamin B_{12}—Vitamin B_{12}-fortified soy beverages and cereals.

Although a vegetarian diet has many pluses, teen girls will want to make doubly sure that their chosen lifestyle is for all the right reasons: animal welfare, environmental protection, and healthy eating—and not for the wrong reasons, like dieting.

If you're already a vegetarian and have any questions on the best food choices to meet your daily requirements, ask your doctor or school nurse.

Ditch the Diets

Crash diets and other quick weight-loss diets don't work. In fact, going on a "diet" usually has a *negative* impact on your appearance, mental alertness, and endurance for sports. The *only* diet you should be on is a well-balanced eating plan that keeps processed food (candy, chips, and

for sports activities. ✪ In 1890, Nellie Bly set a world record with her

soda) to a minimum. You can do this by munching on a variety of good-tasting foods that contain calcium, carbohydrates, fiber, and protein you need (see the Snack Attack box). These foods will give your body strength, energy, and stamina to help you in your sport. So eat and enjoy!

If you think you are overweight and are feeling self-conscious about your body, here are some reasons why healthy eating will bring you better results than dieting and depriving yourself of food:

1. Your metabolism decides how much fuel your body needs. Think of it as your fat burner. Dieting shuts off your fat burner, and exercise turns it on. So if you diet, you actually burn fat less quickly.

2. When you starve your body, your metabolism slows down to protect its stores of fat. So instead of losing fat, your body loses muscle, burning it for energy.

3. When you exercise, you build lean muscle mass. The more muscle mass your body has, the more your metabolism revs up, which burns more calories during *and after* workouts.

Reading this, you might think, "This sounds good, but sometimes when I'm feeling fat, it's just easier to starve myself and exercise more." Okay—reality check! Today there is a dangerous and serious trend growing among athletic girls to eat hardly anything even though they are exercising tons. This is an unhealthy lifestyle choice and can lead to serious eating disorders such as anorexia nervosa (self-starvation) and bulimia (self-induced vomiting). Smart food choices combined with regular exercise and plenty of rest will give your body and mind a sense of peace and overall good health.

72-day, 6-hour, 11-minute unescorted journey around the world by way

Amenorrhea: What Is It?

Amenorrhea means loss of your period for 6 consecutive months or more. For many teens, losing your period for a month or so can be quite common. However, if you don't have your period for more than 6 months, it could be a sign of a more serious problem. Low body fat, lack of essential nutrients, and eating disorders all can cause amenorrhea. In the past, athletic girls and women just took it in stride that they might lose their periods from working out. Some thought that if they began having too many periods, they were not working out hard enough. Today, we know that amenorrhea can lead to bone loss and can indicate other serious health problems. Be sure to talk to your parents or your doctor right away if you have symptoms or are concerned about this condition.

Chapter 4

Body: Year-Round Fitness

Quiz

Injury prone? Take this quiz to find out.

1. Ever since you were little, when you hurt yourself, you:
   a) run for the Band-Aids and a sympathy hug from mom, even if it's just a hangnail.
   b) forget about it; the blood will clot eventually and besides you need to keep up with the guys.
   c) listen to your body and call a time-out to recover.

2. While playing soccer, you charge an opponent who controls the ball. Instead of dribbling around you, she drills the ball right at your bottom lip. You:
   a) freak out at the first sight of blood and run for the first aid kit before you pass out.
   b) keep your cool but ask to be taken out long enough to stop the bleeding.
   c) forget the blood and keep playing, but make a mental note of your opponent's jersey number.

3. You are showing off your bravery to some friends on the high dive, only this time you land a picture-perfect belly flop that knocks the wind right out of you. The first thing you do is:
   a) pretend nothing happened and get right back in line despite the fact that your lungs feel like they've checked out for the day.
   b) take a bow and sit on a bench to catch your breath and allow your cherry-red skin to return to its normal color.
   c) flounder in the water and beg your friends to throw you a life ring.

4. You're riding your bike to your friend's house when you hit some loose gravel and wipe out! When you get up, you see your knee is bleeding. You:
   a) get back on your bike and ignore the blood running down your leg. It'll dry by the time you get to your friend's house.
   b) walk your bike to your house to get your knee cleaned up and Band-Aided before you start out again.
   c) scream as loudly as possible until your mom hears you and helps you home. You call your friend and tell her that because of your tragic accident, you're staying in bed for the rest of the day and can't come over.

5. During basketball practice the girl you're guarding rushes you. Instead of the cool move you had planned to make, you trip over your own foot and fall on the court. When you get up, your ankle is throbbing. You:

gymnast to earn a perfect 10. She received seven of them at the 1976

56

a) tell your coach there's nothing wrong and go back to your position. Hey, you need to make up for that total face plant you just made!

b) let your coach know how your ankle feels, and ask to sit the next couple of minutes out. It's no fun watching from the sidelines, but you don't want to make it worse.

c) limp off the court on the shoulder of your teammate and have the coach call 911. You can never be too careful!

6. You are finally ready to learn how to roller blade. A buddy takes you on what she calls "an easy route." After doing a not-so-graceful tumble down a steep sidewalk, you react by:

a) jumping back on your blades despite the fact that your knees are pretty scraped up—hey, you have a reputation to build here!

b) rip a strip of material from your shirt and tie it around your leg to stop the bleeding from your road burn.

c) take time out to survey the extent of the damage and decide the best way to make it home without another spill like that one.

7. It's the gymnastics tryouts and you are determined to make the team. The first thing you do is:

a) a couple stretches, then gab with some friends about that cute boy on the rings.

b) stretch, then do some warm-up exercises, and then stretch a couple more times—you want to be prepared out there!

c) go straight into your routine—after all, you're not injury prone!

Scoring

1. a- 1, b- 3, c- 2	5. a- 3, b- 2, c- 1
2. a- 1, b- 2, c- 3	6. a- 3, b- 1, c- 2
3. a- 3, b- 2, c- 1	7. a- 2, b- 1, c- 3
4. a- 3, b- 2, c- 1	

21–18 points. Warning! You're tough and you're not going to let a little cut stop you, but you're also prone to ignoring more serious injuries that might need medical attention.

17–11 points. Safety Conscious. You take some chances, but overall you're fairly aware of safety risks and how to prevent injuries.

10–7 points. Oversensitive. Though you can never be too cautious, you may be concentrating more on your injuries than on the game. Remember to also have fun and enjoy yourself!

Part of playing in sports is staying in shape. Even if you can't work out with a team, you can still stay in shape and exercise on your own time. Stretching daily, doing aerobic exercise at least three times a week, and strength training will keep your body strong and healthy all year long. Many of these exercises you can do almost anywhere. So, whether you're on vacation or at home, exercising on a regular basis can enhance your athletic abilities and help you remain injury free.

Stretch Out!

Can you touch your toes or do the splits? If you plan to play sports for years to come, now is the time to get in the habit of doing warm-up exercises designed to stretch your muscles. When your body is stretched and limber:

- you'll be less likely to suffer from strained muscles.
- you'll promote better muscle growth.
- you'll have greater freedom of movement and improved posture.
- you'll feel more relaxed, both mentally and physically.

For each workout session, start and end with stretching exercises that include all the major muscle groups. Cold muscles are hard to stretch and injure more easily. Begin with some low-intensity warm-up stretches. These will help loosen and warm up your muscles before you move into a vigorous aerobic workout. Be sure not to force or overstretch your muscles. Here are a few stretches to get you started.

Common Stretches for Athletes

During all of the exercises that follow, breathe deeply and slowly through your nose, filling up your abdomen first and then your lungs. Exhale fully through your mouth.

woman to swim the English Channel in 1926, beat the previous men's

Body Stretch—Lie flat on your back, arms over your head. Inhale, and stretch your arms and your feet in opposite directions, feet flexed. Hold the stretch 5 seconds. Slowly exhale. Repeat 10 times.

Chest Stretch—Stand up. Clasp both hands together at the small of your back. While still holding hands, straighten your arms and lift them until you can feel a gentle stretch in your chest. Breathe in and out slowly three times. Relax, hands at sides. Repeat 10 times.

Arm and Shoulder Stretch—Stand up. Raise your left arm directly over your head and then bend your left elbow so your left hand rests between your shoulder blades. With your right arm, gently push the left arm so your left hand moves further down your back. Hold that position and breathe slowly in and out three times. Relax. Alternate arms and repeat, 10 repetitions per arm.

Neck Stretch—Sit cross-legged on the floor. Close your eyes. Hang your head down, chin to your chest; hold 5 seconds. Then roll your head slowly back so you're looking up at the ceiling; hold 5 seconds. Turn your head left as far as you can, chin over your left shoulder; hold 5 seconds. Turn your head right, chin over your right shoulder; hold 5 seconds. Repeat the sequence 10 times.

Calf Stretch—Stand, feet together. Relax your shoulders. Step back with the left foot about 2 feet. Keeping both feet on the floor, bend the right knee forward, and stretch the left calf and Achilles tendon (left knee should be bent slightly). Breathe slowly in and out three times. Stand up and relax. Continue, alternating legs, for 10 repetitions per leg.

time by almost __two hours__! ❂ In 1971, they had to make a __law__ in New

Abdominal Stretch—Lie on your stomach and stretch your arms back. Arch your upper body gently back until you feel the stretch in your abdominal muscles. Breathe slowly in and out three times. Lie back down and relax. Repeat the stretch three times.

Lats Stretch—Stand up. Raise your left arm overhead, and grab your left elbow with your right hand. It's okay for the left elbow to bend. With your right hand, pull your left arm toward your head while leaning over to the right. Hold the position and breathe slowly in and out three times. Relax. Alternate arms and repeat, 10 repetitions per arm.

Quad Stretch—Balancing on your right leg, pull your left foot with your left hand to your left buttock until you feel a gentle stretch. Use a chair or wall for balance if you need to. Breathe slowly in and out three times. Put your leg down and relax. Continue, alternating legs, for 10 repetitions per leg.

Back Stretch—Lie on your back. Pull your left knee toward your chest, right foot flexed. Breathe in and out slowly three times. Relax, legs flat. Repeat with the right knee. Continue, alternating legs, 10 repetitions per leg.

Hamstring Stretch—Lie on your back, knees bent and feet flat on the floor. Point your left leg toward the ceiling, or as vertically as you can. Straighten the knee and flex your foot. Stretch more by pulling your leg forward with your hands. Breathe slowly in and out three times. Put your leg down and relax. Continue, alternating legs, for 10 repetitions per leg.

York to allow girls to compete on boys' teams. ✪ Pat Palinkas was the

Hip and Quad Stretch—Stand up, hands on hips, feet apart. Take a big step forward with your left foot, keeping it flat on the floor with toes pointed forward. Bend your right leg slightly and raise the right heel just slightly off the floor. Bend the left knee forward and then try to push your right heel toward the floor. You should feel the stretch in your right quadriceps and the front of your right hip. Breathe slowly in and out three times. Stand up and relax. Continue, alternating legs, for 10 repetitions per leg.

Ready for an Aerobic Rush?

During the off season, when you're not playing regular games or practicing, an aerobic workout can keep you in shape for the next session with your coach. For 20 to 30 minutes, at least three times a week, become your own coach and put your body through some challenging fitness moves. Running, riding your bike, cross-country skiing, and swimming all are great ways to get an aerobic workout. For some aerobic sports that you can do on your own, check out the Solo Sports section on page 21.

Did you know that aerobics can even put you in a good mood? For those times when you're feeling frustrated or angry, a good workout can actually make you feel better. Exercise produces endorphins, a chemical in the human body that gives us a sense of happiness and peace. Plus, who has time for the blues when you're trying to break the jump rope world record?

What's Your Target Heart Rate?

Before you sweat one droplet, you need to complete one mathematical formula—finding out your target heart rate (THR). Your THR is the number of beats per minute at which your heart *should* be beating during aerobic exercise. The best way to tell if you're getting a good workout is to slow down after about 20 minutes, take your pulse, and compare it to your THR. You'll find out if your workout is building endurance and strength, or if you're just plodding along, enjoying the scenery.

To calculate your personal THR you first need to determine your target zone, which is based on your current level of fitness. If you have just started working out and training, you should pick a target zone of 60% or .60. More experienced athletes will want to pick a higher target zone of 70% or .70. After you've established your target zone, you can determine your THR by filling in the blanks below:

220 – ___ (your age) = ___ x .70 = ___ (your THR)

For example, let's say that you're 12 and in great shape. Here's how you'd do your THR:

220 – 12 (your age) = 208 x .70 = 145.6 (your THR)

So what do you do with this THR number? Twenty minutes or so into your workout, slow down and check your pulse. Use your first two fingers (not your thumb) and press lightly on either the inside of your wrist or the front side of your neck. Watching the second hand of a clock or watch, count the number of beats for 15 seconds. Multiply that number of heartbeats by four to get your heartbeats per minute. Get it? Compare this number to your THR. If this number is higher than your THR, you are probably working too hard. If this number is lower than your THR, you may feel energetic enough to pick up the pace or add more resistance (like running up a steep hill) to your workout.

After 20 minutes of aerobics (or more as your endurance builds), decrease the intensity until you're ready to "cool down" with some stretching exercises. Now your body is limber and primed for strength training.

were already woman bullfighters in Spain. ❂ In 1997, Susie Maroney

Endurance Test

Today, take yourself for a jog around your neighborhood. Note your route, so you can repeat it at the end of this test. After your run, write down exactly how different parts of your body feel—example: My lungs are burning up! My legs feel like rubber bands! My heart is going to pound its way out of my chest! Also record your pulse rate and check to see if you're in your THR.

Now continue working out aerobically 20 minutes a day, at least 3 days a week, for at least 4 weeks. At the end of the 4 weeks, repeat the run you made for this test, using the exact same route. Compare how you feel now to what you wrote that first day. Also, check your pulse. Is it closer to your THR than before? If it is, great! That means you are exercising with the safest and most effective heart rate.

Get Buff and Tough

The best time to focus on building and strengthening a specific group of muscles is when your body is warmed up after an aerobic workout. Using the weight of your own body, you can build and strengthen your arms, legs, and abdominal muscles, which will help  you kick a soccer ball further, hit a softball harder, or throw a basketball higher. Strong muscles are also a plus because they actually help protect you when you exercise—they provide support to your joints and can help prevent injuries.

To build muscle, you don't have to visit the gym or lift weights. Strength training also occurs during certain sports activities. Rowing and cross-country skiing target the muscles in your chest, shoulders, back, arms, abdomen, and legs. Additional leg work can come from biking, in-line skating, ice-skating and running.

Strength Training Exercises
That Use Body Resistance

Crunches—Lie on your back, legs straight and together. Put your hands behind your head and roll your head forward until your chin rests on your chest. Keep the small of your back pressed into the floor. Don't pull your head with your hands; let it roll up, with your hands used only for support. Repeat 10–30 times. Do this and you'll have some killer flat abs.

Advanced Push-Ups—Get into a push-up position (either on your knees or on your toes). With a straight back, bend your elbows to lower yourself halfway to the floor. Count to 5, then lower yourself all the way down until your chest touches the floor. Push back up to the halfway position. Hold 5 seconds, then return to your original position. Repeat 3–15 times. Nothing better for arms and chest muscles. Good for back and legs, too.

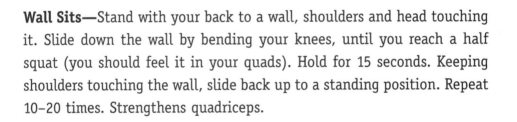

Wall Sits—Stand with your back to a wall, shoulders and head touching it. Slide down the wall by bending your knees, until you reach a half squat (you should feel it in your quads). Hold for 15 seconds. Keeping shoulders touching the wall, slide back up to a standing position. Repeat 10–20 times. Strengthens quadriceps.

Swing Jumps—Stand with your left leg and left arm in front of you and your right leg and right arm back. Slightly bend your knees, and jump up while swinging your arms and legs in the opposite direction before you land. Now your left leg and arm are in back and your right leg and arm are in front. Repeat, back and forth, 20–50 times. Great for arms and legs.

mountain biker, Missy Giove, began racing bikes as a teen, thanks to a

Lunges—Stand up, back straight. Step forward with your right foot as far as possible while keeping your back straight and your left toes on the floor (left heel can come up). Slowly bend your right knee, lowering your body until your left knee touches the floor. Hold 5 seconds, then slowly straighten back up to a stand. Alternate legs, 20–50 times. Builds quadriceps.

Squat Thrusts—First, stand up with your feet about shoulder-width apart. With a straight back, squat down until your hands touch the floor in front of your toes. Next, with hands flat on the floor, lean forward on your hands and kick your feet straight out behind you. Next, with a straight back and legs, bend your elbows and lower your body until your chest touches the floor. Now straighten your elbows to raise your body back up. Then jump back to the squat position while keeping your hands on the floor. Stand up. Relax. Repeat 5–25 times. Strengthens arms, legs, chest, and back.

Arm Rotations—Stand straight, arms extended out. Rotate arms forward in tiny circles. Gradually increase the size of the circles until you are making the biggest circles possible. Do this for 2–4 minutes and feel the burn. Great for arms and shoulders too.

friend's dare. Now she makes ten times more than most pro bikers.

Foot Curls—Stand with bare feet, one foot on top of a paper towel or napkin. Curl your toes to grab the towel, and lift it by flexing your feet, keeping your heel on the floor. Release the towel, and repeat 5–25 times. Works feet, ankle, and leg muscles.

Lateral Jumps—Stand, feet together. Bend your knees to a slight squat and lean slightly forward. Hold your left arm out in front with your right arm behind. Then lean and jump to the right, feet together, while swinging your arms to the opposite position. You should now be to the right of your original position with your right arm in front, your left arm in back, your feet together, and your knees bent in a crouched position. Repeat, back and forth, 20–50 times. This exercise produces awesome leg muscles.

Stair Steppers—You'll need a set of stairs. Be careful; do not run in this exercise. Always place your foot in the middle of the stair and keep your back straight. All of these strengthen legs, ankles, and feet.

1. Walk up and down the stairs on the balls of your feet. Step lightly with little or no impact and noise. (10–20 stairs each way.)

2. Walk up the stairs as in Step 1, but skip every other stair. On the way down, do NOT skip any stairs. (10–20 stairs each way.)

3. Walk up the stairs placing your foot flat on each stair with your heal hanging over the edge and then rising up to your toes to the next stair. Walk down the stairs using the same technique as in Step 1. (25–45 stairs each way.)

○ **The first woman to make the cover of <u>Sports Illustrated</u> (<u>not</u> in a**

Staying Fit

"In the off season I do strength training including push-ups, crunches, weight-lifting, and chest-ups to keep in shape."
—**Gretchen Chomas, age 15, basketball player and discus thrower**

"Volleyball coaches always give us punishments that help us condition. One of my quirks is that I love 'em! If we don't reach a goal on a drill or something along that line, they will tell us to do *bruins*, *burpies*, or get *snoozed*. A *snooze* is when the coach spikes a ball at you. You must dig the ball up . . . roll and get up in time for the next ball coming at you. Although this wears you out, I love it because it pushes me to the limit."
—**Kylie Kenyon, age 12, volleyball player**

"1. Practice hard. At practice give it all you got. Ever hear the saying 'practice hard, play hard?' It's true. You will never excel if you don't practice, and game situations will show you how you've practiced.

2. Play with the boys! You may not win at this all the time, but they certainly will toughen you up.

3. Practice at home on your own! I'm sure you can manage to take 15–30 minutes out of your day to practice by yourself. This time is crucial because you can practice what you need to work on, not what the whole team needs to work on.

4. Stay in shape! This can help you play longer and harder. Even in your off season, stay in shape. You will be a starter when your sport kicks up again.

5. Mentally think over your game! According to the saying 'Sports are 80% mental and 20% physical.' Make goals for yourself to reach. Think all this positive stuff over when you go to bed. This should help you improve and play smarter.

6. Watch professionals play! You will see how to play your sport and play it well. You might need to go to the game sometimes to get firsthand experience."
—**Michelle Meyer, age 12, soccer, basketball, and softball player**

bikini, that is) was diver Pat McCormick in 1952. They showed her diving

Playing It Safe: Preventing Injuries

Certain parts of your body grow at certain times in your life. While these body parts are going through growth spurts, they tend to be especially fragile to injuries. Before you make it to third grade, your heels and hips are growing rapidly. Nine-year-olds need to beware of ankle sprains, since this is a key period of ankle growth. Knees are most injury prone as you enter your teen years.

Most sports injuries occur at the beginning of the season when players are usually out of shape. If you've read the first part of this chapter, you'll know how to get yourself into condition before the first day of practice and avoid those injuries. At least one month before your first practice, start working out three or four times a week. Gentle stretching before and after exercising and at night before you go to bed can help loosen up stiff muscles.

Who wants to be sidelined with an ace bandage on your ankle when your team is about to make the playoffs? The best remedy for sports injuries is prevention:

- Keep yourself limber and strong—strong muscles protect your joints where many injuries can occur.
- Learn the correct methods, skills, and rules in your sport. For example, throwing the bat after hitting the ball is against the rules, shows poor method, and can injure a teammate.
- Wear the right shoes and protective gear.
- Use proper equipment and make sure the playing surface is in good condition—ruts and holes can equal sprains and strains.
- Avoid unhealthy behavior, like smoking cigarettes.
- Get plenty of sleep—this allows your body to replenish itself emotionally and physically.

four stories into a small tub of water. ✪ Over 100 years ago, working-

Overuse Injuries

Teens and preteens who specialize in one sport often suffer from
"overuse" injuries. Rather than a traumatic injury, like a broken bone,
an overuse injury is a repetitive "microtrauma" such as a sore elbow
from practicing pitches over and over for weeks on end. Kid athletes are
more susceptible to overuse injuries like "teenager's knee," "Little
League elbow," "swimmer's shoulder," and "gymnast's back" because
their bones are still growing. To prevent overuse injuries, you can cross
train so you won't overdo it in one sport. If you're a big runner, for
example, cross train in a sport that will work your upper body too. Also,
give yourself a break by making sure you have at least 2 days a week
without any scheduled sports activity.

Taking the time to check in with your body, to note its aches and pains,
can be the best way to avoid an overuse injury. Check out the following
sequence of events. If they seem familiar, you may have a "microtrauma":

1. After a workout, you have sore muscles.

2. Those sore muscles still bother you the next morning.

3. Muscle pain hits you at the beginning of a workout, then stays
throughout the entire workout.

4. Just doing something routine around the house causes you pain.

class French women boxed and wrestled. ✪ Janet Guthrie was the first

If this is you then it's time to take action. Check with your parents or a responsible adult who can help you make an appointment with a doctor specializing in pediatric sports medicine.

Mix It Up!

"Some advice to girls is to try different sports and play them all. I have tried tennis, softball and gymnastics. Mia Hamm played football."
—**Charly Hodges, age 13, soccer player**

Smoke Signals

One of the worst things an athlete can do is start smoking. Did you know that tobacco companies actually target teenagers in their cigarette advertising? They need to recruit at least 5,000 new smokers a day, because that's how many they lose each day to smoking-related deaths like heart disease and lung cancer! And girls are their number-one customer. Just take a good look at the women's magazine ads selling cigarettes. These ads falsely link smoking to independence, fashion, beauty, and slimness. The nicotine in cigarettes is more addictive than the illegal drug heroine. One survey of high school students who were daily smokers showed that only 5% of them intended to be smoking in 5 years. But because they were addicted, 75% of them were actually still smoking 5 years later!

Compare the Body of a *Teen Smoker* with the Body of a *Teen Athlete*

Teen Smoker

Lungs—Underdeveloped, shortness of breath, more often sick with colds, flu, and pneumonia. Produces phlegm twice as often as nonsmoker.

Heart—Rapid heartbeat, beating two to three times more per minute than nonsmoker.

Brain/Mind—More likely to abuse alcohol and illegal drugs such as marijuana, cocaine, and heroin.

Body—Hair, fingers, and breath smell like an ashtray. Teeth are stained yellow.

Life Span—Each cigarette reduces a smoker's life by 5–20 minutes, which can add up to 14 years—gone!

Wallet—$1000 plus per year on cigarettes leaves little money for movies, CDs, clothes, and gifts.

Teen Athlete

Lungs—Strong, clean, and healthy; excellent stamina and endurance.

Heart—Powerful with clear arteries, works efficiently, gets stronger with each workout.

Brain/Mind—Focused, competent, positive, realistic, motivated.

Body—Fully energized, radiating strength and natural beauty.

Life Span—She could celebrate her 80th, 90th, and even 100th birthdays!

Wallet—Plenty of money for sports equipment, entertainment, and plenty of other necessities.

set skating fashion for the next 60 years when she shocked the world in

What is the number-one reason girls first try cigarettes?

   a) peer pressure
   b) to lose weight
   c) to control stress

The answer is "b." A 1998 study found that the number-one reason teen girls start smoking is they believe it will help them lose weight. But amazingly, the study also found that the girls who smoked were 30% more likely than their nonsmoking peers to be overweight! Peer pressure is difficult to avoid, but easy to handle. When you're offered a cigarette, just say, "No thanks—I need to stay in shape for soccer." As for stress, physical activity is one of the best ways to get rid of tension. Next time you're exercising, reflect on a current problem, then use your peaceful workout time to come up with a brilliant answer.

1930 by wearing a short skating dress and matching skates. Women then

Chapter 5

Mind: Relaxation, Goal Setting, Imagery, and Self-Talk

Quiz

Are you down in the dumps or on cloud nine?
Find out how you weather the stormy days.

1. You're grounded, looks like you and your room will be as one. You:
   a) sulk, kick, and complain loudly enough to make sure that your mom in her office can sense your displeasure.
   b) after an initial grumble, dive into *Jane Eyre* and are sorry when you're allowed to rejoin the 21st century.
   c) finally get a chance to rearrange the furniture and make a donation to Goodwill from the childhood relics lurking in the far reaches of your closet.

2. Your teacher announces that she is having a creative drawing contest for your class and the winner gets two free movie tickets. You decide to:
   a) forget about the contest—you can't even draw a circle with a compass.
   b) hand in a doodle from class—you are sure that you could never win but it never hurts to try.
   c) get out your colored pencils and get to work—you may not be Picasso but throw movie tickets into the pot and you're willing to do whatever it takes!

3. You got in trouble in science class for throwing a frog leg at your best bud. Your punishment? Stay an hour after school and pick up all of the trash on the grounds. You feel:
   a) horrified—you're always the one that gets caught and what if your crush happens to see you?
   b) bummed—you promised your friend that you would meet her for a milkshake.
   c) relieved—it could have been a lot worse and, plus, you get to quell your conscience and do a favor for the environment.

4. You get a writing assignment back from your English teacher, and you got a C! The same day, your teacher hands out another writing assignment. You:
   a) throw away the assignment and vow to never write again. It's obvious the teacher hates you, so why should you bother?
   b) don't put much effort into the new assignment. If a C student is what you are, a C student is what you'll stay.
   c) start working on it the minute you get home and make it your best writing ever. You know you can get an A if you try hard enough!

5. Your best friend just moved and invited you to her new house to watch videos. You hop on your bike but even though her directions are clear and easy to follow, you end up in an unfamiliar part of town, and you realize you're completely lost! You finally get to her house an hour late. You're:

didn't even show that much skin at the beach. ✪ In her many travels,

74

a) in a totally bad mood! You can't believe you were so stupid that you got lost, and it has ruined your whole night! You're too upset to watch the videos and end up going home.

b) pretty annoyed at yourself, but after your friend assures you that it's no big deal, you happily help her make popcorn and pop in the movie.

c) fine! You know it's nobody's fault, and you're just happy you could finally find your friend's house.

6. The new movie you've been dying to see came out last weekend, and your dad promised he'd take you. He calls an hour before the movie starts and explains that he has to stay late at work, but he'll take you some other time. You:

a) sit in your room the whole night and pout after getting into a big fight with your sister at the dinner table.

b) call your best bud to complain and then go to her house for some feel-good junk food eating.

c) don't sweat it! You call your friends and make other plans. You know it's not your dad's fault, and the night is still young.

7. Your team just bombed the last play of the championship game and lost! You:

a) go into the locker room with a frown and blame your teammates for the failure. You're sure that if you'd been on a different team, you could have kicked some butt!

b) feel kinda bummed, but keep your mouth shut. Blaming your teammates won't help anything.

c) keep a smile on your face and congratulate everyone! Hey, it isn't every day that you actually make it to the championship. So what if you didn't get the biggest trophy!?

Scoring

1. a- 1, b- 2, c- 3	5. a- 1, b- 2, c- 3
2. a- 1, b- 2, c- 3	6. a- 1, b- 2, c- 3
3. a- 1, b- 2, c- 3	7. a- 1, b- 2, c- 3
4. a- 1, b- 2, c- 3	

21–18 points. Nothing but Sunshine. Your positive outlook on life helps you get through the tough days. Whether you're at a practice or in a competition, seeing the positive side of the situation helps you to be your best.

17–11 points. Partly Cloudy. You're not usually bummed out but once in a while you'll let a discouraging experience get the better of you. Remember that you can always learn from your mistakes to make the most out of any negative situation.

10–7 points. Heavy Showers and a Chance of Thunder. Lighten up! Though things may seem bad at the moment, take time to reflect on the good things that have happened to you, too!

Anna Pavlova was the first person to introduce ballet to such far away

Your physical body executes the moves that score the points, but it's your mind that keeps your body focused and confident. Many athletes couldn't get through a competition without first tapping into their mental game—using relaxation techniques, goal setting, imagery, and self-talk. These mental techniques can *also* be used in other areas of your life. Tests, first dates, class presentations, and band performances are just a few examples of the many ways you can use positive mental skills to improve your performance in almost any situation. In this chapter you'll learn why your mind might be your most important resource in sports, and how, without preparing your mind, your body is just "going through the motions."

Train Your Mind

"I enjoy Judo because I get to learn not just physical power, but also mental power. Our training requires us to be very physically fit, but our coach teaches us that it is just as important to have a strong disciplined mind."
—**Chantalle Castellanos, age 12, judo student**

Ready to Relax?

The crowd is going wild and you feel a rush of excitement and anxiety as you take your place on the free-throw line. Will you make the shot? You look at your teammates, your coach, your parents, and suddenly it seems as if the whole world is watching your every move. As you struggle to calm yourself, you aim for the basket. Taking several deep breaths, you dribble the ball slowly, shoot—and make the perfect shot! Your team goes berserk and you feel great.

What's the secret to performing well under pressure? Relaxation. It helps you focus and improve your performance. Best of all, you can use the relaxation techniques described below for almost any occasion when you

places as Cuba, Costa Rica, Brazil, China, Japan, Indonesia, India,

are feeling stressed. Activities like yoga and meditation can also help you focus on relaxing your body and mind.

Breathing

One of the quickest ways to relax your body and your mind is by changing your breathing. Many people don't notice that their breathing rate increases as their anxiety and stress levels go up. Here are some simple steps to calm yourself and create some inner peace before the next big game:

1. Find a quiet, comfortable spot and close your eyes (unless you're in the middle of a game).

2. Take 10 deep breaths. (Don't do more than 10—we don't want anyone passing out!) Enjoy each inhale and exhale.

3. Think about things that make you happy and relaxed like playing with your dog or going to the movies with your friends.

4. Open your eyes and let the newly relaxed you do what needs to be done.

Muscle Relaxation

Besides deep breathing, these muscular relaxation techniques can also help prepare your mind and body for competition:

1. First, pick one muscle to focus on. If you're a softball pitcher, you might want to start with a muscle in your pitching arm. A soccer player might want to start with a muscle in her legs or feet.

2. Close your eyes and breathe deeply.

3. Focus your mind on this muscle. Imagine all the tension in it flowing out and away from your body.

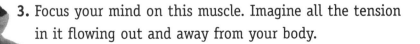
Egypt, and New Zealand. ✪ Virne "Jackie" Mitchell was the first woman

4. As you begin to feel yourself relax, move on to a new muscle in the same area. Allow your mind to help this muscle relax, too. Continue until your entire body feels relaxed. Soon you should start feeling more at ease and ready to face your fears.

Get the Stress Out!

"Tae Kwon Do is a beautiful and graceful sport! It helps to keep you fit and flexible. It is a great way to work out your aggressions as well as a terrific stress reliever! (Perfect for any girl with teen stress.)"
—**Sarah Kingery, age 12, Tae Kwon Do student**

Setting Personal Goals

The big day is here! You're about to run the city marathon, something you've been preparing for over the last 3 months. Though this is your first marathon, you are ready and confident. The race starts. At first you feel good, but as the day's heat and humidity begin to suck you dry, you start to lag. Then you remember the goal you set for yourself, to finish the marathon no matter what. Realistically, you can't keep the same pace and achieve your goal. You ease up and make sure to grab some extra water from the next check point. Before you know it, you've finished the marathon, and a huge feeling of accomplishment washes over you.

Goal setting is a great way to keep your priorities straight and block out distractions during competitions and events. By defining goals for yourself, you can more clearly envision what you may need to work on. Many people who use goal setting feel less stressed out, are more focused, and are more satisfied with their performances. Here are some simple steps to positive goal setting:

to play for an all-male pro baseball team in 1931. She even struck out

1. Create a positive statement for yourself. For example, "I will improve the efficiency of my swim stroke." instead of a negative statement like "I will try not to swim so slowly."

2. Use dates, times, or other concrete ways to measure your goal. A bowler might want to reach a score of 120 in the next two months. Using actual numbers and dates will help you to define exactly what your goal is and help you to determine if you've achieved it. Once you determine the details of your goal, write them down so you won't forget them.

3. Be sure not to make your goal too large, like "I want to go to the Olympics for skiing next year." when you've only skied twice in

Go for the Goal!

"Since second grade it has been my goal to break the mile record at my school. The record was set in 1989, the year I was born. Every year, I dropped at least 20 seconds from my time. This year, as I started the fifth grade, I trained with my dad to run the mile. I kept thinking while I was running, 'I'm gonna get it! I'm gonna get it! Come on push!!' When I crossed the line, I was exhausted. My gym teacher said, 'Excellent, Megan, your time was 6:36!' I shouted with joy! I finally had the record by over 20 seconds!"
—Megan Mischler, age 10, track and field athlete

"Don't let anyone tell you that you can't. Can't isn't in my vocabulary. I try everything. You don't have to be the best athlete to participate in sports. You just need to want to do it. It may not seem fun to wake up at 4 a.m. to go out running in the middle of the summer (because it's too hot to run any later), but once you get going it's all worth it."
—Cassie Kipper, age 14, triathlete and runner

baseball legends Babe Ruth and Lou Gehrig. ✪ There is evidence that

your life. Your goal should be small enough that you will feel it is achievable. Once you've achieved it, set another goal.

4. Don't be discouraged if a game or performance doesn't go as well as you planned. Goal setting is about acknowledging yourself for the good work you've put in and all the small improvements you've made along the way—not about being the best every time.

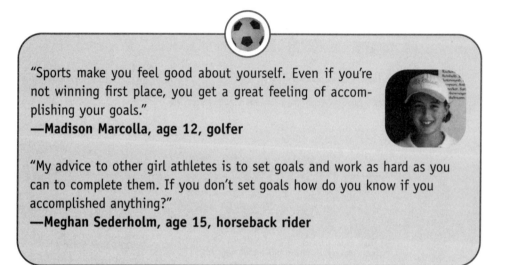

"Sports make you feel good about yourself. Even if you're not winning first place, you get a great feeling of accomplishing your goals."
—Madison Marcolla, age 12, golfer

"My advice to other girl athletes is to set goals and work as hard as you can to complete them. If you don't set goals how do you know if you accomplished anything?"
—Meghan Sederholm, age 15, horseback rider

Imagery

You're skiing and your instructor just took you to her favorite run on the mountain. Only thing is—it's covered in icy moguls! It's your worst nightmare. Visions of going down the mountain face first streak through your mind. As your instructor and the rest of the class wait for you at the bottom, you realize these negative thoughts aren't really helping the situation. You take a moment to close your eyes and imagine executing a perfect run, delicately avoiding the moguls and using your edges to cut through the ice. Suddenly, you feel much better and make your way down the hill—mistake free!

a Spartan princess, Cynisca, was the first woman to ever win an

See how imagery works to help your mind throw out negative thoughts? Just like exercise keeps your body in shape, imagery is a workout for your mind, mentally preparing you for future athletic events. By thinking over a situation and imagining successful sports scenarios, you train your mind and body to work together more harmoniously. The more you practice imagery, the better you'll get at solving specific problems like improving the arc of your golf swing, or more complex problems like calming your fears at the top of a ski run. And on days when your body isn't up to speed—maybe you're injured, exhausted or the weather is too nasty—imagery can help you practice your sport in your mind.

Though you can use imagery at any time, the best time to use it is when you're relaxed and feeling calm. Here are some tips to keep in mind as you use imagery to visualize success:

1. Think of a sport scenario, like an upcoming meet, a workout at practice, or a skill you would like to improve upon.

2. Imagine *all* the details of that scenario: the smell of the gym (we know—kinda gross, but it works!), pool, or playing field; the feel of the basketball, soccer ball, and other equipment you might use; the sounds of your coach, parents, friends, and teammates.

3. Using these real-life details, imagine how you might feel during this event or activity and add these feelings to your scenario.

4. Focus on the work your hands, legs, and body must do to perform successfully.

5. Imagine yourself going through the motions of your sport and achieving success by your actions. Let yourself feel good about your accomplishments. Now that you've achieved success in your mental workout, you're ready for the real thing!

The Mental Game

"My advice that I want to give to other female athletes comes from a quote about baseball, 'You can't possibly hit the ball if you are thinking about all the possible ways you can miss.' Like most sports, volleyball is half mental. A coach and a friend taught me that if I think how I can better myself and keep telling myself I can do it, I can do anything my heart desires."
—Kylie Kenyon, age 12, volleyball player

"The advice that I have for other girl athletes is that no matter how small you are (I'm only 5 feet tall), great things come in small packages. I've always been one of the shortest girls on my team, but it didn't stop me from trying to do my best. To believe you can is everything!"
—Abby Wolfe, age 14, basketball player

Self-Talk

You're playing soccer and you have 30 seconds to score before you go into "sudden death." You urge yourself on, "Come on! You can do it! You can get the game-winning goal!" You shoot, you score!

It might sound a little crazy but self-talk it a great way to get yourself jazzed up and ready to give your best throughout a game or event. As an athlete, you might have days when you've lost all confidence in your abilities. By using self-talk, you can chase away discouragement and bring back self-confidence.

Being honest with yourself plays a key role in helping to improve your skills and confidence in playing sports. But often we only tell ourselves the *bad news* and never point out to ourselves the *good news*. You *need* to counter your negative thoughts with positive ones. Positive thoughts and affirmations can help repair the damage that negative thinking has done to undermine self-confidence.

Your own affirmations should be based on fact, the things that you are good at, such as achieving your goals or learning from your mistakes, or a skill you have that's unique to your sport. Here are some examples to get you started:

"I can throw a softball straight and hard."
"I am positive and energetic in practice and games."

Write your own affirmations here:

_____

_____

_____

_____

_____

Each night, before you shut off your bedside lamp, read your self-affirmations out loud. And if your little brother catches you "talking to yourself," just include one last affirmation, "I am patient enough to love my little brother no matter how annoying he is!"

Inner Strength

"When I first started I was a bad player . . . my teammates told the coach to kick me out. I felt sad until one day I decided to talk to the coach privately and told him to show me how to kick and hold the ball with my legs. He told me 'You gotta play from your mind and your heart, not just with the ball because courage and proudness is what makes you hit the ball and score.' On my next practice, I remembered the words from my coach and played. By the time the ball came to me, a little voice inside my mind said 'Play from the heart and mind.' I was so concentrated on the game that I knew for the first time how to move and pass the ball without falling."
—Analy Casillas, age 14, soccer player

"My favorite quote from Mia Hamm, that I will remember and respect for the rest of my life is 'I have worked too hard, and too long to let anything stand in the way of my goals. I will not let my teammates down, I will not let myself down.' That just gets me pumped. For games only, I put a picture of Mia Hamm in both of my socks, for strength and courage and for good luck."
—Tori Nichols, age 12, soccer player

Getting the Team Psyched

You can even talk to your coach about getting your whole team involved in "energizing activities." If she agrees, these are some techniques that can pump up your whole team:

1. Increase "high five's"—slapping the hands of your teammates gets everyone's blood circulating.

2. Talk to each other during drills and practice—shout out encouraging statements and give helpful feedback.

a foot to protect them from <u>overexertion</u>. ○ Jean Balukas was the first

3. Use positive signals like eye contact, a "thumbs-up," and clapping when a job is done well.

4. Play high-energy music to liven up your practice and pregame warm-ups.

Team Spirit

"We were undefeated and playing the second-hardest game in the league, and right as the referee blew the whistle I knew it was going to be a hard and tiring game, by the fourth quarter they were winning 5-3. I was thinking ... this calls for some desperate measures. So my friend gave me her lucky Halloween wig, and the other team started laughing at me but I didn't care what they thought. I knew we had a chance to win this game. We actually tied the game, leaving us undefeated and the other team totally mad."
—Krista Droze, age 13, soccer player

"We played our game hard, but lost. While we were talking, two of my friends and I got the Silly String and sprayed the coaches and the entire team. We had a lot of fun after that game. Maybe we had lost on the field, but we were still winners!"
—Maya Hunt, age 12, soccer player

"As a starter, I'm expected to pump up the team and get morale going even when we're down. And trust me, if you ask my teammates, they'll tell you that it's pretty easy for me because I can be really, really loud!"
—Katie Peska, age 15, volleyball player

Chapter 6

Spirit: Staying Up When Others Are Getting You Down

Quiz

Do you suffer from communication breakdown?

1. Your dad can't help himself. He comes to your soccer game and yells enthusiastically at you to kick, to block, to run, to ATTACK!!!. Duh . . .You:
   a) glare at him from the field after every outburst and hope he'll get the message.
   b) turn bright red and hope that no one knows he's your dad.
   c) pull your dad aside, tell him thanks for coming to your games, but please knock off the armchair quarterbacking. It's distracting you from the game.

2. It's a rainy day and your best friend suggests that the two of you hit the bowling lanes. The only problem is that every time it's your turn she tells you that you're doing it wrong. It's driving you insane! You:
   a) tell her to zip it and start aiming at the gutters just to make her mad.
   b) tell her thanks and joke that until you see her holding a championship trophy in her hand, she'd better step aside and witness some beginner's luck.
   c) don't say anything; she'll just get mad, and you can at least try to zone her out.

3. You're watching your favorite TV show, when your mom, who's usually totally mellow, comes home from work in a bad mood and yells at you for leaving your coat on the couch. You:
   a) yell back and leave your coat on the couch. What's up with her?
   b) hang up your coat in the closet, make your mom a cup of tea and ask her what's wrong.
   c) try to ignore your mom until she goes away—you're watching TV!

4. During basketball practice, one of your teammates starts making fun of you every time you miss a shot. You try to ignore her, but soon she has some of her friends in giggles over your dribbling. You:
   a) grab some of your friends and point out what big feet the other girl has, and how bad she is at guarding. Two can play at this game!
   b) keep ignoring her and hope she'll stop. Practice only lasts a half hour more, you'll survive.
   c) walk over to the girl when she's alone and ask her straight out why she's bugging you. If that doesn't work, you set up a meeting with the two of you and the coach to get things straightened out.

Championship. ○ When she was at the University of North Carolina, Mia

5. You're at the mall with a friend and every time you tell her you like something she tries it on and then buys it! You are thoroughly annoyed so you:
   a) stop speaking up when you see cute stuff.
   b) yell at her for copying everything that you do and vow never to shop with her again.
   c) gently tell you how you are feeling and offer to treat her to a frozen yogurt.

6. It's the first day of soccer practice and your best friend who begged you to join has completely ditched you to cling to the star center. You:
   a) quit the team and stomp off the field. She's the reason you joined in the first place, and if she's ditching you, you'll return the favor.
   b) hang in there and, after practice, tell her that your feelings are hurt. Who knows? Maybe she didn't even realize she was ignoring you.
   c) keep quiet and pretend you're having fun, even though you don't know a soul on the team.

7. Your coach takes you out of the game right after you just scored a killer lay up. You:
   a) kick your chair and give your coach dirty looks until the end of the game.
   b) wait until the game is over and ask your coach why you were taken out right after making a good shot.
   c) sit silently at the end of the bench wishing that your coach would stop ignoring your talent.

Scoring

1. a- 3, b- 1, c- 2	5. a- 1, b- 3, c- 2
2. a- 3, b- 2, c- 1	6. a- 3, b- 2, c- 1
3. a- 3, b- 2, c- 1	7. a- 3, b- 2, c- 1
4. a- 3, b- 1, c- 2	

21–18 points. Whoa! Take a deep breath—nothing's worth getting that angry over. Besides, blowing up at someone before telling them what they have done wrong can hurt feelings, and it's just not fair to the other person.

17–11 points. Calm, Cool, and Collected. You're great at sharing your feelings without making other people feel bad. Keep up the good work and you'll find that your relationships will continue to be open and honest.

10–7 points. Speak Up! After all, your feelings count too. Know that your problems are important enough to be addressed. If a teammate, parent, or coach doesn't agree with your point of view, at least you know that they are aware of the situation and of how you feel.

Hamm scored more goals than any other player in college soccer history—

Just as your body does the physical work and your mind keeps you focused, your spirit keeps you involved in sports even through the difficulties. Miscommunication or hurt feelings is one of the easiest ways to get your spirit down. If you're going to be an athlete, you need to learn how to cope and communicate to keep your spirit up.

What if during a soccer game, you accidentally blocked a shot your teammate was making, sending the ball haywire? Next thing you know, the other team has control, tramples down the field and gets a goal! You feel rotten. And the girl whose shot you blocked yells at you for the mistake! Her anger makes you want to just quit the team. Hold on a minute! If everyone would calm down and talk it out, feelings could be spared and maybe a lesson would be learned.

Positive Communication Techniques

Communication means to "share with others," or, in other words, to express what you feel and hear what others have to say rather than have a screaming match. If you're facing a person who's angry at you and saying unkind things, by choosing your words carefully, you can cool down tempers. Having a two-way conversation brings understanding like, "Oh yeah, now I get your point!" Here are a few suggestions to help get you on the path to positive communication:

Learn to Listen—In order to communicate positively with someone else, you must not only know how to communicate your own feelings effectively, but to listen to how other people are feeling too. For example, if a teammate is telling you why she is mad, don't interrupt. Wait until she is finished then tell her your perspective. Try to pay attention to what she is saying (even if you don't agree), to not interrupt, and to ask questions or rephrase what she has said so that she knows you are listening.

male or female. ○ **Shannon Dunn, two-time World Half-Pipe**

Use Positive Body Language—Keep your body language posi-
tive with eye contact. Your tone of voice should also be positive,
calm, and reflective. Half of communication is what you say, the
other half is *how* you say it.

Avoid the Blame Game—Once you've established your listening skills
and expressed positive body language, you're ready to deal with the
really tough issues. Be sure to concentrate on the problem at hand
(rude, discouraging, mean behavior) and *not on the person*. Address the
behavior that is bothering you and why. Use phrases that begin with
"I feel..." instead of "You did this..." so that you can speak honestly
about your feelings and, at the same time, avoid blaming the other person outright.

"Use 'I messages' like, 'what works best for me is when you pass me the
ball from the left...'"
> Jim Thompson
> *Director, Positive Coaching Alliance*
> *Stanford University*

Dealing with Other Players

One of the most frustrating and nerve-racking encounters you can have
in sports is being teased and taunted. Girls from out-of-town teams
might harass you during a scuffle on the field. Or maybe it's someone on
your own team who is giving you a hard time. No matter whose mouth
these insults are coming from, it can be painful. When cruel words are
thrown your direction, they are aiming for two things: your self-confidence and to get a reaction from you. There are several steps you can
take to protect your self-confidence and keep yourself positive.

If you're faced with someone who is calling you names or putting you
down, it's okay to feel sorry for them. Negative people are generally

Snowboarding Champ, personally painted the new graphics for her

unhappy about stuff going on in their own lives and often express themselves by cutting down others. This is because they feel so poorly about
themselves they want others to suffer too. Because the person who's
insulting you is hoping to get a reaction, ignoring them often works as
a way to prevent further confrontation. Try not to answer attacks with
some choice words of your own—this will only prolong the shouting,
and more ugly words will be said.

Sometimes, other players or teams will intentionally use taunts and
insults to distract you from your game. Since their plan is to defeat you
using any means possible, don't let their insults get the better of
you. Focus on your game and remember, they're the ones with something to worry about.

Keeping Your Cool

No one likes being accused of things that are untrue. Your natural reaction is to set the record straight. If ignoring the person doesn't work and
the teasing goes on, you may want to say something eventually and use
your positive communication techniques to turn things around. The following are some examples of what *to* do and what *not* to do if you suffer from a communication breakdown.

Communication Breakdown

You're playing basketball and a teammate criticizes you for missing an
"easy" play:

Freak Out Response—Yell "At least I CAN play!" and proceed to steal
the ball from her every time she gets a pass, even though she is on
your team.

Consequence—You'll probably get yanked by your coach and most likely ruin any chance to get along with that teammate again, not to mention looking like a moron in the process!

Cool Response—Say, "Let's stay positive and talk about mistakes after the game."

Out on the field, a girl from the opposing soccer team yells an insult about your bright orange-and-green team uniform.

Freak Out Response—You turn a clean game of soccer into a nice tackle football game.

Consequence—Red card, you're out of the game! And we're pretty sure that you'd have to get used to the view from the sidelines for a while.

Cool Response—A simple, "Thanks, I love our school colors." should make her feel pretty small, and you can keep your head in the game.

Your older brother starts teasing you about not being a starter.

Freak Out Response—Vow to "START" sticking up for yourself and drill him in the jaw.

Consequence—You can bet that your parents will hear about it, and you've probably just started a painful rivalry with your bro.

Cool Response—Ignore the teasing. If you can't, tell your brother that a starter position is a big deal, and you're working on it.

A parent from the opposing team makes fun of you and your teammates for messing up.

Freak Out Response—Run into the crowd during a time-out and threaten to plant the ball right between his eyes.

Consequence—You look pretty silly standing in the crowd threatening an adult. Your coach gets the idea that your head isn't in the game and benches you.

Cool Response—During a time-out, ask your coach or a ref to have that parent keep it down.

helped organize and sponsor the benefit Boarding for Breast Cancer.

Staying Positive in Sports

"My advice to any girl who wants to play any sports is to have fun and a positive attitude, no matter what."
—Eva Rodriguez, age 13, basketball player

"Some advice I have for other athletes is:
1. Don't let anyone discourage you!
2. Believe in yourself.
3. Do what makes *you* happy, not what someone else wants you to do.
4. Don't be intimidated into thinking you're no good."
—Katrina Cusack, age 12, basketball player

"My most memorable gymnastics experiences are probably from my first meet ever. I forgot my floor exercise routine and got a 3.0 out of a 10.0, but then, the same year, I went on to win the State Championship on the floor exercise."
—Alyson Cobb, age 12, gymnast

"I never received an award for playing tennis, unless you count the plaque that all the team members received, or the certificate saying that yes, I really was on the team. But the experience of playing tennis—the really good feeling that I get when I make an amazing serve or get my backhand just right—is rewarding enough for me."
—Dana Willbanks, age 14, tennis player

"Some of my experiences have been good and some of them bad. Once last year I was in a competition against other teams and I was doing my singles routine. I was very nervous. I was messing up on all my tricks and my coach was one of the judges. I ended up not winning any prizes, but I was still upbeat and was glad for my other teammates. This year I plan to enter both competitions and try my best to jump for joy, not for winning a prize."
—Kayla Cornett, age 10, rope-jumper

✪ **Elizabeth Buggy was the first girl to compete in the national finals of**

Dealing with Parents

Sometimes the hardest people to deal with in sports are the parents. At times, even getting your parents interested in helping you learn to play a sport can be difficult. Many parents worry about the financial obligation of sports, how to get you to and from practices and games, and if the sport might take up too much family time or distract you from school. If these are problems you face, try to organize a plan for playing sports that deals with these issues. Look into school-sponsored sports programs that offer after-school buses to take you home from practice. You can also create a schedule, illustrating how you will balance family obligations and homework with your sport.

Overprotective Parents

Often, girls have a hard time convincing their worried parents to let them play sports. What if you break your leg while skiing? Or end up with a concussion after your forehead meets a field hockey stick? These concerned parents are highly protective and just want their daughters to be safe rather than sorry. But "safe" can be boring. Sports are exciting, fast paced, and full of friends and fun. What are the magic words that will convince a paranoid parent to give the "thumbs-up"?

Since your mom and dad's priority is your safety, show them written material about the safety features in your sport. If you want to join the field hockey team, ask the coach for a field hockey handbook that lists the rules and regulations. Included in this book would be safety equipment such as shin guards, helmets, proper shoes, etc. If your sport has a code of ethics that shows how players must treat each other during games and practices, this will help your parents understand that sports are not just madness and mayhem.

the NFL Punt, Pass, and Kick Competition. She finished second in the

Adults talking to adults might do the trick. Ask the field hockey coach to give your parents a phone call. This way, they can ask an "expert" specific questions that will hopefully throw away any lasting fears they have.

Over-Involved Parents

Are you experiencing some heavy pressure from your parents to always win, even though you're happy just playing sports for the fun of it? Is your dad the guy who is always getting in the ump's face accusing him of a bad call? Is that your mom screaming insults at the coach of the visiting team?

If you can relate to these experiences, your games are probably packed with more embarrassment than pride. It sounds like you need to help your parents manage their tempers, their mouths, and their cheering techniques before one of them gets thrown out of the stadium, or you end up bummed enough to quit.

Many parents realize that girls today have more sports opportunities than they had. Though Title IX has changed things for you, some parents might try to live vicariously through your sport experiences because they were denied the opportunity to compete in sports when they were young.

Before you bring up the subject of their behavior, review the positive communication techniques listed earlier in this chapter. Your parents will probably end up respecting your opinion, your positive approach, and your calm demeanor. By bringing up the following points, you might also be able to show your parents your perspective:

12-year-old age class. ✪ In 1971, tennis legend Billie Jean King became

96

1. You play sports for one main reason—to have fun. When your parents are screaming and yelling insults from the stands, this takes the fun out of sports for you, and makes you think about quitting once and for all.

2. Just as you have a role on the team and are responsible for your actions during games, your parents have roles and responsibilities. Verbal insults teach kids it's okay to use name-calling when dealing with others.

3. You hope to play sports for years to come. Now is the time to build good relationships with the league and coaches. The last thing you want is for you and your parents to have a bad reputation within the league. This will only hurt your chances of playing in the future.

4. Remind your parents that playing sports is a great way for you to learn about leadership, motivation, self-confidence, and keeping fit. Winning and losing are not nearly as important.

Parent Pluses

"Sports have helped my relationship with my dad especially because we get to spend a lot of time together."
—Delaney O'Brien, age 12, softball and basketball player

"It helped my parents become more active because they would throw the ball with me and help me practice batting. They like to go to games. I didn't have to convince my parents to let me play softball. If my dad tried to give me too much advice I would just tell him to calm down."
—Kristen Wahlquist, Age 9, softball player

the first woman athlete in any sport to earn more than $100,000 in a

Once you've gotten over these communication hurdles and have told your parents where you're coming from, you will see that sports can actually help your relationship with your parents.

Dealing with Discouraging Coaches

One of the hardest jobs you may ever have in sports is keeping your spirit alive while playing for a discouraging coach. Coaches who use fear tactics, practice public humiliation, or ignore you can make it difficult to enjoy or even want to play a sport. Unfortunately, these coaches are rarely corrected because parents and girls don't want to make the situation worse. And girls don't want to make their coach more angry for fear they'll lose their spot on the team. However, there are ways to effectively deal with discouraging coaches and create a positive outcome for everyone involved.

Talk about It

"I find I can usually talk my problems out with my coach and he takes what I say seriously. Another thing I might do is go talk to an assistant coach or teacher about problems I am having and they can go talk to the coach for me."
—**Carrie Cravalho, age 17, cross country, track and field, and basketball**

"One thing you could do is talk with the other girls on your team and see how they feel about the coach. Most important is just to talk and release your own tension so you won't feel stressed."
—**Jessica Wahlquist, age 12, soccer and softball**

single season. ✪ **Before her famous game against ex-champ Bobby**

"Pick a time to talk to your coach when she will best listen and hear what you're saying. Also, tie your needs into the coach's goals, 'You'll get my best effort if you. . . .'"

Jim Thompson
Director, Positive Coaching Alliance
Stanford University

Your Coach Practices Public Humiliation

Was there ever a time when you double-faulted your tennis serve and lost an important match? Or maybe that time the volleyball was set up for your spike, but you overpowered it right into the net? How did your coach react to these mistakes? If she jumped all over you, screeching all your faults for everyone to hear, this is probably a scene you wish could be wiped clean from your memory bank. A 1997 Canadian study found that 25% of kids laying sports had been verbally abused by their coaches. Not too many girls are going to stick it out with that kind of encouragement.

Crummy Coaches

"My first teacher gave me the skill of performing with presence and flare. Using innovative strategies and music, she instilled more and more love of the dance in my heart. If it hadn't been for that, I may not have continued, because when I moved into the higher level class with a different teacher, I almost gave up. My new teacher didn't like me from the beginning. She would constantly call me names like 'Ms. Jellyfish' and the 'Class Elephant.' If I made one wrong move she would ostracize me. It only took a little while to deplete my self-esteem, but no matter what she did, my adoration of ballet carried me through. After two years of putting up with crying almost every night after dance, I took a friend from school's offer to take a ballet class at her studio. It only took me a single class to know that was where I would have the most fun dancing."
—Victoria Sandbrook, age 14, dancer

Riggs, Billie Jean King had to "get comfortable with the idea of beat-

"When a girl messes up, it's okay! I don't need to keep telling her what she did wrong. A girl who's dedicated will probably never make the same mistake again."

Huan Phan
Coach, CYSA soccer team

Coach Communication

A coach who instills fear or embarrassment in you can quickly break your spirit. The best way to handle this type of coach is privately. Have your parents make an appointment with the coach where you can meet behind closed doors. Yes, this meeting can make you a nervous wreck, but isn't that what you already are during every practice and every game?

A great way to psych yourself up for the meeting is by *role-playing* with your parents or friends. This is like doing a skit where you talk out a situation or problem. Role-playing can really help you prepare for the unexpected or the unknown. While you talk it out, you can find answers or solve problems that might have seemed impossible before.

Sample Role-Playing Script

Have a parent or friend "play" the role of your coach, and you "play" yourself.

You: "Coach, I feel like you've been giving me a lot of negative feedback lately and I'd really like to know if there is anything I'm doing right."
Coach: "Well, if I don't tell you what you are doing wrong, how are you going to know what you need to work on?"
You: "Sometimes it helps to point out the mistakes but it also helps me to know what I'm doing well. Those times you've pointed out a good play I've made have really helped my game."
Coach: "Huh? . . . I don't remember doing that."

ing a man." She got comfortable with it and beat him badly. ۞ Cristen

You: "Yeah, it was some of the best coaching I've ever experienced!"

Coach: "Oh sure, now I remember."

You: "Everyone says positive reinforcement and strong encouragement are the best ways to keep girls in the game—and you have a knack for doing just that!"

Coach: "Well thanks, I'll keep in mind what you said. Now let's get out there and have some fun!"

Dealing with Coaches Who Ignore You

If you are feeling neglected or ignored by your coach, don't drop out just yet. This is a common problem many kids face. Sometimes when there are lots of kids on a team, it may be hard to get the individual attention you need to improve your game. You might try getting a few pointers from your coach after practice, when she is less busy. If this doesn't work, ask her if an assistant coach could help with team training (an older team member or even a parent might be able to volunteer for this role).

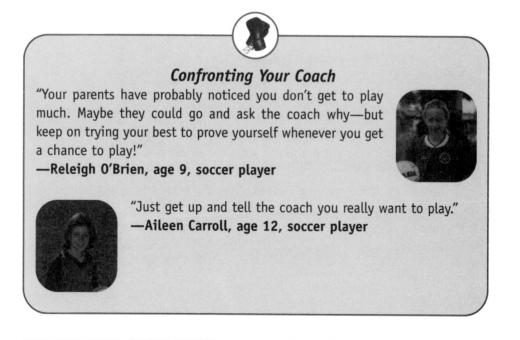

Confronting Your Coach

"Your parents have probably noticed you don't get to play much. Maybe they could go and ask the coach why—but keep on trying your best to prove yourself whenever you get a chance to play!"
—**Releigh O'Brien, age 9, soccer player**

"Just get up and tell the coach you really want to play."
—**Aileen Carroll, age 12, soccer player**

Powell's Top Fuel dragster victory in 1997, when she was 18, made her

What if your coach still places you in the same position and doesn't let you try anything new? You might ask her how to improve your game so that you can move to a different position. She may not even know that you're dissatisfied with the position you have, or you might even find out that she has a special reason why she wants you in that spot. Whatever the case, after talking to her, she'll know your needs and you'll also have a better understanding of where she is coming from. More than likely, she'll be willing to help you improve your game by mixing up the positions a little.

Caring Coaches

Even though you might have some difficulties with your coach, through positive communication you can make the most out of the player-coach relationship. Great coaches can inspire you even if you don't win, can encourage you to try your hardest for yourself and your team, and can bring a team closer together. Most coaches want you to be your best. Here's an example of how good communication can bring you closer to your coach:

Caring Coach

"My favorite coach is definitely my cross-country coach. He earns your respect but also knows when you're having an off day and he gives you your space without letting you slack off too much. I always know that, when I have a problem either with cross country or life, he is constantly backing up my decisions no matter what."
—Carrie Cravalho, age 17, cross country, track and field, and basketball

How to Throw Like a Girl When You're Playing with the Guys

Sure, some guys are uncomfortable playing sports with girls, but you can help them get over it! Make them go slack jawed as they watch you bat a ball over the head of the center fielder. By the time you stamp on home plate, they'll be hoping to be on the same team as you! Here are some girls with great advice on how to "throw like a girl" when you're playing with the guys:

Beating the Boy Blues

"One funny thing that happened to me was at one of my games. After seeing my ponytail sticking out of the back of my helmet, a guy from the other team said to one of his teammates, "Look, that guy has a ponytail!" One of my teammates just laughed at him. Don't let anyone tell you that you can't do it, especially boys. The boys who tell you that are probably worried that you'll be better than them."

—Cody Blackburn, age 13, roller-hockey player

"Many sports, like hockey, are dominated by males. It is not fair if you are rejected for being a girl. Take a stand, not only for yourself but all girls. Many accomplished female athletes were told that they couldn't play because they were a girl. They took a stand and look where they are now, Olympic Gold Medalists."

—Melissa Sailor, age 12, ice-hockey player

Pavlova and her ballet company once danced for 30,000 fans inside a

"I do lots of sports but football is my favorite. The best part about being the first and only girl in football is that the boys expect you to do things wrong, but when you show them that you can do it and they can't, then you feel proud of yourself. Before the first game we had to pick names for the people we wanted to be our captains. To my surprise they picked me and three other people."

—Ayla Brown, age 11, football, basketball, and soccer player

"I used to be harassed because I play on an all-boys hockey team. What made it even worse is that I am a goalie. The kids on my team would harass me and even some parents too. Sometimes it would be weeks before anyone even spoke to me. All that has changed now because I've proved that I'm not the enemy and am just as good, sometimes better, than any guy on the ice. I spend more time at the rink than with friends. But that's okay because the guys on my team ARE my friends. If there was any advice I could give to other girl athletes, it would be to never give up your dream and always work your hardest, and never forget—GIRLS GOT GAME!"

—Alli Smith, age 12, ice-hockey player

"My advice to girl athletes is if you are on an all-boys team or you feel you don't fit in, stick with it and make happen what you believe you can do. My most memorable experience occurred when . . . I hit my first home run ever! All the boys were proud of me. Afterward, I was awarded the game ball."

—Sarah Gold, age 11, baseball player

"My only choice was to play on the boy's soccer team (and what's worse, my brother's)! At the first practice I was pretty nervous. Everybody knew each other except for me. When we paired up to do passing, the only one who would be my partner was my brother, and he grumbled a lot. Nobody passed to me during the scrimmage. My coach was very supportive of me being on the team (and he passed to me). The day for our  first game arrived. I was again fairly nervous and I fell down a lot. It was rough. Finally I scored and all the moms went wild! I scored two more goals and we won 4-1. As the season went on, I even earned the confidence of the boys on my team. They even passed to me, *occasionally*."
—**Jessica Curtin, age 15, soccer player**

"Just because you're a girl, some people are going to think you can't be an athlete. Ignore them, girls are just as good at sports as boys are. As my favorite poster says, 'You run like a girl, you jump like a girl, you swing like a girl, you tumble 6 feet over a 4-inch beam LIKE A GIRL.'"
—**Alyson Cobb, age 12, gymnast**

"I asked the boys at school if I could play soccer with them at recess. At first, the boys did not like to pass the ball to me. Now they know that I am just as good as they are, and most of the boys treat me like a regular teammate. I know that just because I am a girl doesn't mean I can't play as well as the boys."
—**Megan Johnson, age 7, soccer player**

"My favorite rivals are boys because they always think that they are better, stronger, and more fit than girls; and I love proving them wrong."
—**Jennifer Layton, age 12, soccer player**

player to win a grand slam singles event in over 100 years, and the

Chapter 7

Scholarships and Careers for the Sports-Savvy Girl

Quiz

Are you headed for the WNBA or will you be reporting on it? Discover your future in sports.

1. You're watching the WNBA on television. After the game, you call up your teammate to:
   a) give her a play-by-play of the action.
   b) go over your strategy for next week's game.
   c) plan a postgame party.

2. You love rules and making sure people play a fair game. You're a problem solver who would rather work:
   a) on the basketball court.
   b) in the courtroom.
   c) on the sidelines.

3. You see yourself as a:
   a) team leader, out on the court setting an example.
   b) moral supporter, encouraging girls to participate in sports.
   c) team manager, helping to organize games and meets.

4. You just watched the final in women's tennis at Wimbledon. You wish you could have been:
   a) the player who won it all.
   b) the coach who gave her the good advice.
   c) the agent who convinced her to go pro.

5. Your team is hosting a v-ball camp for little girls and your coach is handing out jobs. You ask to:
   a) help the girls work on their serves.
   b) scrimmage with your other teammates to demonstrate proper form.
   c) post ads all over town to recruit more girls for the camp.

youngest woman to be ranked number one in the world. ○ Sonja Henie

6. You're on your way back from practice and you see a group of young girls playing softball. Your first instinct is to:
   a) go over and give them some pointers, and maybe pitch them a couple of balls so they can practice their swing.
   b) join in the game—you want to be part of the action!
   c) sit and watch for a couple of minutes. Maybe you'll see a great player you could encourage to join a league!

7. Your little brother is practicing his jump shot and you notice that he has a horrible follow-through. You:
   a) run out and challenge him to a game of H.O.R.S.E.—hey, he needs the practice and you love to win!
   b) plan a family H.O.R.S.E. competition, complete with winner's brackets and a trophy.
   c) walk up to him and ask if you can give him a little tip to help his shot.

Scoring

1. a- 3, b- 2, c- 1   5. a- 2, b- 3, c -1
2. a- 3, b- 1, c- 2   6. a- 2, b- 3, c -1
3. a- 3, b- 2, c- 1   7. a- 3, b- 1, c- 2
4. a- 3, b- 2, c- 1

21–18 points. Professional Athlete or Sports Reporter. When you're aren't playing the game, you're talking about the game. Your dream job would be to somewhere in the thick of the sports action.

17–11 points. Sports Coach, Trainer, Therapist, or Psychologist. You like sports so much that you want everyone around you to get a chance to play their best. You dream job would be one where you can pass on your love of sports to others.

10–7 points. Agent, Lawyer, or Administrator. You can't keep sports out of your head and you've always been good with handling money. Your dream job would combine your business skills with your favorite sports.

was the first woman figure skater to incorporate ballet moves and

Do you ever close your eyes and imagine what your future holds? Maybe you see yourself going to college on a sports scholarship, continuing to improve at your sport as you play at national levels of competition. Or possibly a career as a professional athlete is what you have in mind, where you can get paid to play the sport you love. You might even decide to go into a career like coaching so you can train and inspire other athletes.

Sports Scholarships

Usually, the first step to a career in sports is college. Though college can be expensive, many colleges offer sports scholarships that can reduce or pay for tuition. Getting a sports scholarship is a great way to get on a college team, combine your love of sports with your future goals, and improve your sport skills.

Besides looking at your athletic abilities, colleges will also look at your grades, test scores, writing, and outside interests (like volunteering, jobs, or club activities). The National Collegiate Athletic Association (NCAA) Initial-Eligibility Clearinghouse also has a list of requirements for anyone interested in participating in Division I or II intercollegiate athletics. To participate at the college level, the NCAA Clearinghouse requires that you:

- graduate from high school.
- earn at least a 2.00 grade-point average.
- score at least an 820 on your SAT.

For more details on these standards, contact the NCAA Clearinghouse at:

NCAA Clearinghouse
PO Box 4044
Iowa City, Iowa 52243-4044
Phone: (319) 337-1492
Web: www.ncaa.org

jumps into her routines. Before her, skaters just traced figures in the

Picking Your School

To make sure the school you're interested in is right for you, see if it's excited about athletics, supports women's sports, and has a good academic reputation. The following are a few of the top colleges in the country that support women's sports.

Top Colleges for Women Athletes

(Based on championships won, varsity club and intramural opportunities, graduation rates, financial aid, facilities, traditions, and attitudes.)

Abilene Christian University	www.acu.edu
Bloomsburg University	www.bloomu.edu
College of New Jersey	www.trenton.edu
Duke University	www.duke.edu
Harvard University	www.harvard.edu
Middlebury College	www.middlebury.edu
Old Dominion University	web.odu.edu
Pennsylvania State University	www.psu.edu
Princeton University	www.princeton.edu
Stanford University	www.stanford.edu
State University of NY, Cortland	www.cortland.edu
University of Arizona	www.arizona.edu
University of California, Davis	www.ucdavis.edu
University of California, LA	www.ucla.edu
University of Connecticut	www.uconn.edu
University of Florida	www.ufl.edu
University of Georgia	www.uga.edu
University of Maryland	www.maryland.edu
University of Nebraska	www.unl.edu
University of North Carolina	www.unc.edu
University of Notre Dame	www.nd.edu
University of Tennessee	www.utk.edu

ice during competitions. ✪ Women began playing basketball in the late

University of Texas	www.utexas.edu
University of Virginia	www.virginia.edu
University of Washington	www.washington.edu
University of Wisconsin	www.wisc.edu

How to Get an Athletic Scholarship

Here are three ways you can win an athletic scholarship:

1. A touring coach will find you herself. Lucky you! Many coaches go on the road to search for talent, attending high school games and meeting with high school coaches. If you are invited by a coach to play for her college team, you will still need to apply to the university through its admissions department. Make sure you receive a contract that provides the details of the scholarship offer.

2. Call a coach yourself. If there is a school that you feel is just right for you, find out who the coach is in your sport, and contact her directly. However, be prepared to prove your achievements. Were you voted MVP last season? Do you have a videotape showing a game in which you rushed three defense players to score a winning goal? Check the web site of this university for the results of recent games in your sport. Compare its statistics to your own. The more you know about yourself and the school, the better you're going to look to a coach.

3. Look up resources for scholarships on the web, at your public library, or at local bookstores. It may seem overwhelming at first, but you'd be surprised how many people (librarians, teachers, book-store clerks, your parents) will be willing to help you in your search. Here are some books and web sites to get you started:

1800s. ○ In ancient Greece, there was an Olympic competition for

Books on Scholarships

Foundation Grants to Individuals, by Phyllis Edelson.

The Athletic Recruiting and Scholarship Guide, by Wayne Mazzoni.

Peterson's Sports Scholarships and College Athletic Programs, edited by Ron Walker.

Athletic Scholarships: Making Your Sport Pay, by David Lahey.

College Admissions for the High School Athlete, edited by Theresa Foy Digeronimo and Jack DiSalvo.

Web Sites on Scholarships

National Collegiate Athletic Association	www.ncaa.org
College Athletic Placement Service	www.capsplacement.com
College Scholarships	www.collegescholarships.com
College Net	www.collegenet.com
General Information Regarding Athletic Scholarships	www.ftclondon.co.uk/athsch.htm
College Prospects of America	www.cpoa.com
Female Athletic Recruiting	www.allsportsconnection.com
Women's Sports Foundation	www.womensportsfoundation.org
Athletes Edge (Student Athlete Recruiting)	www.athletesedge.com
American Association of University Women	www.aauw.org/home.html

women called **Heraia** in honor of the goddess Hera. ❂ More than

Academic Athletes

"I want to play soccer for my high school and college years, and maybe even get a scholarship."
—Tori Nichols, age 12, soccer player

"I realize that getting good grades is important to possibly getting a scholarship so I try my hardest in school also."
—Michelle Meyer, age 12, soccer, basketball, and softball player

"I attend a private, college prep school and have been told many times that I would have to drop some of my sports to keep up academically. I am happy to say that I am proving that girls can be athletic as well as smart! And I have not dropped any of my sports!"
—Chantalle Castellanos, age 12, judo student

Careers in Sports

Sports have become a *60 billion dollar* industry, which adds up to tons of sports-related careers and opportunities. Not only can you choose to be a coach or a P.E. teacher, but you could also study to be a sports psychologist or a sports administrator. You can find degrees in these fields at many colleges and universities. For girls who want to be professional athletes, doors have been opened that were once bolted and padlocked. Today, girls can get paid to be race car drivers, cyclists, equestrians, figure skaters, skiers, golfers, bowlers, beach volleyball players, rock climbers, surfers, tennis players, water skiers, triathletes—just about any sport you can imagine, you could get paid to do it!

There are over 6 million jobs in sports-related careers. Many of them are listed in *Careers for Sports Nuts and Other Athletic Types*, by William Ray

650,000 fans attended the Women's World Cup soccer games in 1999

Heitzmann. Here are just a few of the many sports-related careers out there. Maybe one of them will be in your future?

Athletic Trainer

Job Description—Specializes in the prevention, treatment, and rehabilitation of sports-related injuries.

Educational Requirements—A bachelor's degree in exercise and sports science, CPR and National Athletic Trainers' Association certification.

Pay Range—$25,000 to over $60,000.

For More Information Contact:

National Athletic Trainers' Association

(214) 637-6282

www.nata.org

American Council on Exercise (ACE)

(858) 535-8227

www.acefitness.org

Coach

Job Description—Gives athletes instruction during practices and games. Oversees and evaluates athletes' development. Administrative tasks include budgeting, scheduling, and recruiting staff and athletes.

Educational Requirements—A bachelor's and/or master's degree in physical education.

Pay Range—$15,000 to $200,000.

For More Information Contact:

National Women's Coaches Association

(615) 974-7281

www.nwcawebsite.org.

National High School Athletic Coaches Association

(800) 262-2495

hscoaches.org

(and millions more watched it on TV), making it the most popular

Exercise Physiologist

Job Description—Evaluates and suggests training and fitness programs that will improve an athlete's performance. Recommends rehabilitation treatment for injuries.

Educational Requirements—A master's degree and board certification are required.

Pay Range—$18,000 to $75,000.

For More Information Contact:

American College of Sports Medicine

(317) 637-9200

www.acsm.org.

American Physical Therapy Association

(703) 684-2782

www.apta.org

American Orthopedic Society for Sports Medicine

(847) 292-4900

www.sportsmed.org

Fitness Instructor

Job Description—Provides instruction and personal training in sports and exercise.

Educational Requirements—A bachelor's degree in exercise and sports science with a certificate in training.

Pay Range—$20,000 to over $200,000.

For More Information Contact:

Aerobics and Fitness Association

of America

(818) 905-0040

www.afaa.com

Physical Education Teacher

Job Description—Gives instruction and positive reinforcement to students in sports and recreational activities. Plans classes, gives lessons, and administers tests that teach the skills and rules of team and individual sports. Works with individual students and evaluates their performance and potential.

Educational Requirements—A bachelor's degree, state licensing, and completion of training programs are required.

Pay Range—$20,000 to $37,000.

For More Information Contact:

American Federation of Teachers

(202) 879-4400

www.aft.org

Sports Administrator

Job Description—Oversees university sports programs. Acts as a mentor to school athletes. Handles sports marketing, development, training, and information for colleges and universities.

Educational Requirements—A bachelor's degree in business or sports management.

Pay Range—$15,000 to $300,000.

For More Information Contact:

National Association of College

Women Athletic Administrators

(910) 793-8244

www.nacwaa.org

doing gymnastics moves, and dancing on tombs dating back to 2134 B.C.

117

Sports Agent or Attorney

Job Description—Handles legal questions and business arrangements regarding sport issues for athletes, teams, leagues, conferences, civic recreational programs, educational institutions, and other organizations involved in professional, collegiate, Olympic, and amateur sports.

Educational Requirements—A law degree and bar certification, plus additional knowledge in the type of sports law you wish to specialize in.

Pay Range—$30,000 to over $1,000,000.

For More Information Contact:

National Sports Law Institute

(414) 288-5815

Sports Journalist and Broadcaster

Job Description—Reports on any sports-related stories, from accounts of actual games to individual teams and players. Jobs range from writing for newspapers and magazines to reporting for local and national television stations.

Educational Requirements—A bachelor's degree in journalism or English, and experience working for a college newspaper as a sports reporter.

Pay Range—$20,000 to over $500,000.

For More Information Contact:

American Sportscasters Association

(212) 227-8080

www.americansportscasters.com

Newspaper Association of America

(703) 902-1600

www.naa.org

Sports Official

Job Description—Ensures that a game is played by the rules, emphasizing fairness and safety.

Educational Requirements—A high school diploma; at a higher level, state certification.

Pay Range—$15,000 to $250,000.

For More Information Contact:

National Association of Sports Officials

(414) 632-5448

www.naso.org

Sports Psychologist

Job Description—Suggests treatment for athletes to help them improve performance. Gives athletes stress management techniques and helps them overcome motivation and concentration problems.

Educational Requirements—A master's degree and/or a doctorate in psychology, and state certification/licensing is required.

Pay Range—$20,000 to $100,000.

For More Information Contact:

Association for the Advancement of
Applied Sport Psychology
www.aaasponline.org
American Psychological Association,
Sports Psychology Division
(202) 336-5500.

Future Aspirations

"My most memorable event was making the USA Power Tumbling Team. After I competed at the team trials, I was ranked 3rd in the United States for my age group. The top four were named members of the USA Power Tumbling Team and we got to travel to South Africa to compete against girls my age from all over the world. It was awesome!!! My advice to other young athletes is to stick with it and maybe your dreams will come true. My dream is to make it to the Olympics. I hope I do!"
—Janelle Knutti, age 11, power tumbling

"When I tell people I want to play on the USA Volleyball team, they look at me like I'm nuts and laugh in my face. But I know if I practice hard and do my best every time I'm on the court, I will reach my goal!"
—Sara Snyder, age 12, volleyball player

male or female, to free-climb The Nose in Yosemite National Park, one

Should I Have a Career in Sports?

Before you head out the door to apply for that job as a sports commentator, take this quiz:

Write on this line the career in sports you want:

_____

Now, using a scale of 1–5 (1 being the weakest, 5 being the strongest) answer the following questions on your chosen career:

1. How strong is your determination to have this career?_____

2. Knowing your talents and skills, how well do you think they would help you in this career?_____

3. How excited are you knowing that you have four years or more of college to learn about your chosen career?_____

4. Looking back on your *favorite* classes, school projects, and sports experiences, have you already proven to yourself that this career could be in your future?_____

5. Would you be willing to volunteer your time in a job in your chosen field to learn more about your career?_____

Is this the career for you, or do you need to switch gears?

25–21 points. Go for it! Your talents and traits make you a shoe-in for this career.

20–11 points. Do a little more homework. Find out more about the skills and education needed before you make a 100% commitment.

10–5 points. Working in a sports career might seem exciting on the surface, but underneath maybe it wasn't what you expected.

Future Aspirations

"This is the first year Tae Kwon Do will be recognized as an official Olympic sport. I am hoping to be able to represent the United States in the 2004 Olympics as a competitor in Tae Kwon Do."
—Sarah Kingery, age 12, Tae Kwon Do student

"I admit that I may not be the best girl soccer player out there; I'm no Mia Hamm. But if I keep practicing, or if anyone keeps practicing hard enough, and is dedicated to a sport, I believe I can get up to that level, bit by bit. It takes heart, soul, but most of all it takes love of the game."
—Jennifer Layton, age 12, soccer player

"I want to major in Athletic Training. I've always wanted to be an athletic trainer and get out and work with athletes like football players."
—Taylor Adkins, age 11, basketball and softball player

"Don't let things get in the way of your ambitions and dreams. You only live once so live it to your fullest."
—Melissa Wegner, age 15, basketball player

ity that makes them feel best about themselves is athletics. YOU GO GIRL!

Chapter 8

This Could Be You!
Real Women Talk about How
Sports Changed Their Lives

We hope this book has inspired you and made you proud to throw like a girl! You've read about girls who struggled and triumphed against discouraging words, injuries, and their own jangling nerves. They've dealt with unreal coaches, taunting boys, and overbearing parents. They've practiced, they've sweated, they've cried, they've cheered, and in the end they got the best reward: pride in themselves. Now they know they can do it—whatever *it* happens to be: sports, schoolwork, conflicts with families, friends, or teachers. Sports have given these girls skills to cope with all the curveballs life can throw.

You've taken the quizzes, you've read our advice, you've figured out which sport is for you. We hope you'll remember, when you get out there on the field, on the slopes, in the water, or on the court what you learned in this book. Throwing like a girl means eating and exercising smart, psyching yourself up, and dealing positively with parents, coaches, and teammates. But most of all it means you are in the game!

But there's one more thing. For that last little bit of inspiration, check out these stories of ten successful sports women. These women had many different struggles as girls: seriously ill parents, prejudice against girl athletes, even debilitating injuries. But one thing they all have in common is that they gave their sport—and their lives—100% intensity and dedication. This group of sports women includes a pageant winner, a surgeon, a sports administrator, a WNBA star, and several Olympic medalists. The lessons they learned in sports brought them to the top of their fields. Even if they never pick up another ball, ski another mogul, or catch another wave, they're winners for life.

Woman of the Waves

Sarah Gebhardt
*Graduate Student in Physical Chemistry
and World Class Surfer*

When Sarah turned 3 years old, her mother, who was suffering from muscular dystrophy, became confined to a wheel chair. Even little Sarah had health trouble. Her allergies would trigger intense asthma attacks. Sarah's life was made more difficult when her parents separated. Caring for her mother and coping with school and a broken family, Sarah did her best to handle the pressure and responsibilities, but eventually something had to give. When the stress became overwhelming, Sarah's asthma hit full force. She had to be hospitalized.

Despite all the difficulties, Sarah knew she had a goal in life: to discover a cure for muscular dystrophy so that her mother could get better. But to do that, she needed to improve the straight D's she was earning in school. "In junior high, I tried out for the basketball team," says Sarah, "I had never played a team sport before, but I was tall and lanky, so the coach signed me up." After that, things got better. Sarah's grades improved, landing her name on the honor roll. "Playing a sport was an incredible turning point for me. As a member of a team, I worked harder to better myself so I wouldn't let anyone down. It was a very supportive group of people—our coach was great about giving us positive feedback."

At 14, Sarah decided to try surfing for the first time. She dragged the bulky board into the water and pointed it toward the horizon. She began to paddle with her hands, straining every muscle in her body. Her neck was cramped and her arms were on fire. But Sarah was determined to ride.

Sarah had her ride and it changed her life. She discovered that surfing fit perfectly with her independent spirit. "There is a stereotype of surfers being slackers," she says, "but surfing requires strength, timing and agility. There is no way you can be lazy and a daydreamer and still be a strong surfer." Sarah's parents were very supportive of her love for the sport. Her dad bought her a surfboard and her mother encouraged her to use it.

Surfers chase after their waves, and to find them, Sarah has traveled to Hawaii, Brazil, Australia, and Indonesia. In California, Sarah has surfed the "Mavericks," giant waves whose very name suggests rebel, misfit, renegade. Photos of Sarah riding those towers of water have appeared on web sites and in sports magazines across the country.

The only people who challenged Sarah's presence on the waves were other surfers—all guys. "The guys gave me a hard time. They felt it was their sport, so they excluded me. I became angry because all I wanted was to learn from them. My mom set me straight. She told me to fulfill my dreams, and not let their attitude get in the way of what I wanted to do." Sarah took her mother's advice to heart, and at 25, she is not only one of the world's best female surfers, but she has also pursued her love of sciences, and will soon have her Ph.D. in physical chemistry. "To find the cure for muscular dystrophy, I needed to study biology. But my first chemistry class was fun and I understood it, so my goals changed." Sarah believes that being in a male-dominated sport has helped her in a male-dominated career. She has proven to herself that she can solve difficult scientific problems, or ride walls of water just as well or better than the men around her.

I Love It, So I'm Going to Play

Cammi Granato

Captain of USA Olympic Women's Hockey and Gold Medalist

If Cammi Granato had paid any attention to the many adults who told her "You shouldn't be playing," she would not have an Olympic gold medal hanging around her neck. Instead, Cammi was always a key player in the furious games of hockey she and her four older brothers held in the basement of their home. The five kids had a solemn agreement between them: Don't tell mom if Cammi took too many bumps!

Despite the risk of losing a tooth or two, Cammi says, "My parents were always supportive of me playing hockey. A lot of parents thought it was silly I was out there playing with the boys. It did make me feel self-conscious when I would walk into a hockey rink and people would stare and snicker at me." Not many people would continue in the face of such hostility, but Cammi knew she was good. "I was playing hockey for the love of it, and I had no idea that I was any different than the boys. I didn't care if I was a girl, I just wanted to be the best. And I especially didn't want to listen to people tell me 'sorry, there's no future for you.' Heck, I planned to play with the guys when I grew up, and that meant playing for the Chicago Blackhawks."

Cammi attributes much of her success in hockey to her brothers, especially Tony, now a professional hockey player and a former Olympic team member. Cammi's brothers set high standards for themselves in sports, and Cammi strove to match their talents.

In 1998, Cammi and the rest of the American women's hockey team electrified the Nagano Winter Olympics. They made Olympic history by becoming the first gold medal champions in women's hockey. Out on the ice, the women athletes displayed finesse, superior skill, and a genuine team camaraderie. Cammi says, "Just being involved on a team has given me so much happiness, valuable lessons, and good friendships. The whole concept of everyone working toward the gold medal, made us totally depend on each other. We gave of ourselves and stayed so in tuned with each other. It taught me how much you can accomplish as a united group."

Today, Cammi credits hockey with giving her the confidence to tackle life, leaving self-doubt behind in the dust. "Sports gave me confidence to be friends with guys and to be able to relate to them without being intimidated. I had crushes on guys too, but being involved in hockey gave me a common ground with them. Hockey helped me overcome shyness which might have inhibited me later in life."

Cammi cautions girls whose lack of self-confidence makes them cut down fellow teammates. "It's a mistake to cut somebody else down. Instead, you should work hard to be a better person so you don't have to make others feel less adequate than you. Also, if someone is cutting you down, realize that it's not you—it's the other person feeling bad about herself." And as Cammi would like to remind girls everywhere, "Believing in yourself . . . will get you further than you can ever imagine. Have a passion for your sport, and get involved. Women are kind in team sports. Someone will reach out to you and take you in—that's the nature of women and of our team spirit."

I'll Never Give Up Playing

Donna Lopiano, Ph.D.
Executive Director, Women's Sports Foundation

As a little girl who wanted to be pitcher for the New York Yankees, Donna Lopiano was never told that she had an impossible dream. When the Little League tryouts came to town. Donna, along with dozens of boys, showed up on the field. All afternoon the coaches watched in stunned amazement as Donna whipped pitch after pitch over home plate. She was the number-one draft pick.

Later that day, after all the kids were assigned to teams, they waited in line to get their uniforms. "This was a very exciting moment," Donna recalls, "Since the age of five, I had thrown 500 pitches a day, and there I was, an 11-year-old girl, ready to receive my first baseball uniform." They were navy blue and white, surely this was a sign she would one day play for the Yankees.

"When my uniform was handed to me I could hardly breathe, I was so excited." The happiness would not last. As Donna describes it, a "big tall father" bent down and said to her, "See this rule book? I think you need to give me back that uniform." And he was right. There on page 14, were the words "No Girls Are Allowed." "I was devastated," says Donna, "I was not allowed to play with my friends at what I did best." Donna's parents tried to find a league for girls, but nothing existed. Donna was not discouraged—she knew she would play for a team someday.

When Donna was 15, her dad invited one of his old army buddies to dinner. He was also a scout for the Pittsburgh Pirates baseball team. Donna's ears pricked up when she heard him say he was good friends with the coach of the National Champion women's softball team in Stratford, Connecticut. The scout soon found himself agreeing to bring Donna to tryouts for the Stratford softball team.

A week later, he drove Donna to the ballpark for tryouts. After seeing Donna throw a few pitches, he realized the girl could play! When Donna finished her tryout, the Stratford coach put his arm around the scout and loudly proclaimed him the best in the business. The next year, Donna traveled around the world with the Stratford team, playing games in Hong Kong, the Philippines, Berlin, and Australia.

After Donna graduated from college, she was ready to find a job. Since pitching for the New York Yankees was still impossible, she accepted the position of Women's Athletic Director for the University of Texas. Her first day on the job she found herself in charge of a program that barely existed. But during the next 18 years, Donna built the women's sports program.

"We took a 16,000 seat arena and sold it out for women's basketball. We proved that our athletes could be great athletes and still have 3.0 GPAs and 95% graduation rates. We did all the things men's sports said could not be done." When Donna looks back, she understands that she helped shape women's sports into a dynamic force enjoyed by hundreds of thousands of fans today.

Winning Isn't Everything

Jade Smalls
1999 Miss Illinois and 1st Runner-up in the
1999 Miss America Pageant

The ball was hers, and the floor was open. At the other end of the court, Jade Smalls could see her target—a rim, a net, and the sparkling glass of the backboard. She dribbled fast, knowing this time she could do it. She was tall enough and strong enough. She was going to "slap the glass."

Beneath the hoop, Jade reached up, ball in one hand, the other hand poised to make her hand print for all to see. The ball sliced through the net, and Jade did a pounding high five into the glass. When her feet hit the floor, pain flooded through her thumb. "It was excruciating," Jade says, almost wincing at the memory, "And can you believe I had just been handpicked to play a solo piece with the Charleston Symphony Orchestra the next week?" The jammed thumb was going to make hitting the right piano keys a true challenge.

The night of the performance, Jade's thumb was throbbing. She had only been able to practice one time for the greatest opportunity of her life. Before she stepped on stage, Jade prayed her heart out. She sat down at the giant grand piano and began to play. She played for 13 minutes and 45 seconds. To this day, she describes it as her best performance ever. She took her bow, the curtain fell and her thumb turned into fire.

Jade admits that she never had a "fear of failure." Her father was a civil rights activist, and his experiences taught Jade determination and perseverance. "I am not a competitive person," says Jade, "I play sports and the piano and participate in pageants because I love to perform. This has helped to strengthen my self-confidence, and now I find that I am not easily intimidated."

Even the worst experience she had playing sports taught Jade that winning is not the most important goal. "My girlfriends on my middle school basketball team were so close. We never lost a game, and spent all our free time together." But when they graduated to high school, Jade and her teammates had a radically different basketball experience. Their new coach used punishment and bullying to communicate what she wanted. Every game they played, they lost. "Her methods were like none we'd ever dealt with before. But since playing was what we cared most about, we stuck it out."

In her high school senior year, Jade entered and won her first pageant, becoming Junior Miss Charleston, South Carolina. A year later she won the title of Miss Illinois. Then in 1999, Jade was crowned 1st runner up in the Miss America Pageant. "Just like in sports, where I played so my abilities could shine, being in the Miss America Pageant allowed other parts of my personality to shine," says Jade reflecting on her second-place finish, "Winning is not my ultimate goal. I'd rather take advantage of the platform the pageant gives me and give a message to teenagers at risk."

When she was 17, Jade lost a close friend to suicide. Being a high profile pageant contender has allowed Jade to speak out on teen suicide prevention. Now she serves on the board of the American Foundation of Suicide Prevention. Jade says, "Life is a privilege, a gift, and a blessing. Knowing myself and how much I love keeping active and playing music, I can't imagine wasting a minute of this life God gave me. And that's what I tell teens across the country—use your life, don't fling it away."

Let Your Talent Shine

Dot Richardson, M.D.
Orthopedic Surgeon and Olympic Women's Softball Pitcher, Gold Medalist

One sunny day in Orlando, Florida, 10-year-old Dot Richardson was throwing pitches to her older brother at a local baseball field. When a man wearing a coach's hat ran over to her and asked her to play on his Little League team, Dot thought her life-long dream to play baseball was coming true. In her hometown, only the boys played team sports— girls were not welcomed.

So, as Dot stood looking up at this kindly man who had just invited her to play on his Little League team, she could hear a voice in her head, "This is it! I am going to pitch for a Little League team! Unbelievable!" But then, in his next breath, the coach said, "You're going to have to cut your hair short, and we'll give you a boy's name, let's see, guess we'll call you Bob." Dot was crushed. No matter how much she loved the sport and dreamed of being a baseball player, Dot felt being true to herself was even more important. So, as she stood in her field of dreams, Dot looked up at the baseball coach who was just trying to find a way for her talent to shine. "Sorry," she told him, "but no thanks."

That same day, for the second time in a few hours, another man approached Dot. When he told her what a great arm she had, Dot said to herself, "This is not happening!" The man urged Dot to talk to the head coach of the softball team playing nearby. As Dot walked toward the dugout, she noticed not a single boy on the field—the players were all women!

After fielding and throwing six times, Dot was invited by the coach to play for her team. Dot's mom and dad gave their approval and she became the team's youngest player. Since everyone else was 24 years or older, Dot really had to prove herself. She did. At the end of the year, she made the all-star team. She had just turned 11.

One week before the all-star game, Dot was playing in the backyard swinging from a tree limb. She jumped onto the hood of an old car, and lost her balance and landed on a sharp metal sickle. It sliced through the arch of her right foot and took 15 stitches to close. She had to sit out of the big game.

Not playing in the all-star game was a tremendous disappointment. But Dot looked at her bandaged foot and decided to turn the bad experience into a stepping stone. She hobbled over to the instructional league for the Orlando Rebels, a women's fast-pitch, major softball team, and signed up for trials. That winter, she played the instruction league and earned the title of Orlando Rebels bat girl. Dot was in her glory. For a year she picked up bats and practiced catch with her idols— the Micky Mantles, Babe Ruths, and Lou Gehrigs of professional women's softball. When she was named to the team and became the youngest player ever, Dot knew that dreams do come true.

Dot Richardson is now an Olympic gold medalist, having won as pitcher with the women's softball team in Atlanta in 1996. She is also a medical doctor and surgeon. Dot freely admits that she was born with a gift—the talent to pitch. But just having the talent is not enough to fulfill your dream. Dot worked hard to perfect her skills as a pitcher. She struggled through injuries, mistakes, and put-downs. She never gave up. She turned bad moments into great endings and always practiced harder to be the best she could be.

The Desire to Compete Makes Her a Woman of "Firsts"

Lesley Visser
ABC Sports Commentator

For 20 years, the girls who played field hockey for South Hadley High had not won a single game against their rival, the Sun Two Regionals. Year after year the Regionals crushed the South Hadley Tigers. The sophomore team of 1972 knew this legacy of loss had to end, and it was up to them to change history.

It was an afternoon game, an even game of tug-of-war. Both teams had legacies at stake, so the struggle to score and defend continued between the evenly matched players. Everyone on the sidelines wondered if the puck would ever rocket into one of the goals.

Then, South Hadley team captain Lesley Visser, stick in hand, feet stomping down the grass, saw her opportunity. She got the puck and zigzagged across the field, eyes narrowed, calculating where she needed to be. The goalie loomed large, and the puck seemed to shrink, and two defense opponents were charging straight at her. With a pulverizing smack, Lesley connected puck to the net for a goal. The game ended in a tie and South Hadley was sent into the celebration stratosphere. Lesley remembers being voted Best Athlete, but it was the pride she felt for her teammates and the thrill of competition that she carries with her today. "Playing sports really prepared me for the world beyond school. Out here in society, you cannot escape the competitive games people play. Knowing firsthand how exciting a real game can be, just made me work harder to meet my goals."

Her love of sports guided Lesley into a career where she is paid to watch people play. In 1976, working for the Boston Globe newspaper, Lesley was the first and only woman to cover NFL football as the beat writer assigned to the New England Patriots. Since then, Lesley has witnessed close-up and firsthand major league baseball, the NBA, the U.S. Open Tennis Championship, the Olympics, and she was the first woman to handle the postgame presentation ceremonies at the Super Bowl.

In order to excel in her job, Lesley had to fine-tune her skills of observation. She had to do more than just talk about an incomplete pass or an error in the outfield. Lesley's determination to bring the fans into the game was accomplished by her reporting on the human story behind a player's jersey number. Perhaps this is why Lesley was voted the Outstanding Women's Sportswriter in America and why she won the Women's Sports Foundation Award for Journalism.

"I am not afraid to compete," says Lesley remembering those early years when she was the only woman in the sports department. "Whenever we took a break from reporting to play a game of basketball, it was just me and the guys." Being the only woman doing locker room interviews proves that Lesley is not easily intimidated—a quality she says comes from confronting challenges like the day Lesley and her teammates at South Hadley High broke their losing streak in field hockey.

Don't Let Fear in—Think Positive

Picabo Street

1996 Olympic Skier, Gold and Silver Medalist

The 5-year-old girl was not happy being left behind while her big brother went to go do something called "skiing." Rather than cry and moan, the little girl quietly found an old pair of skis and began practicing in her backyard. Her dad could not help but notice his daughter's struggle to prove herself. So one day he took her up in a real ski lift. At the top of the hill, the little girl hardly stopped to catch her breath before she sent herself over the edge. Dad was far ahead and she wanted to catch up. She didn't look left or right; she just sped straight to the bottom. From that day on, Picabo Street knew she needed to race with the wind.

Maybe it was her upbringing that made Picabo a believer in herself. Her family never owned a television, and Picabo was kept busy with a long list of chores each day. Although her parents were "free spirits," they made sure their two children knew the meaning of hard work and self-discipline. When she was ten years old, she told her dad she would race in the Olympics one day. Her dad respected her dream and encouraged her to make it happen.

But speed skiing is a dangerous sport. Skiers have been known to reach speeds as high as 110 miles per hour. When they crash at those speeds, there's bound to be pain and injuries. In her years as a racer, Picabo has crashed and burned many times. She's dealt with concussions, blown-out knees, and broken legs. But amazingly, these scary experiences have only helped her to conquer her natural fears of the unknown. "When you're ready to start something, you can think about the bad things that can happen or the positive things. You have control over yourself both mentally and physically. When you plan for a positive outcome, you're able to go for it."

Picabo admits to having fears before she races. But she uses visualization techniques and positive thinking to energize and motivate herself. Each time something bad happens to her, she turns it into a positive lesson. "Just before the Olympics in Nagano, I was skiing down a mountain in Sweden, barely moving at 60 mph." In midturn, one of Picabo's skis fell off. She spun around then crashed head first onto the hard-packed powder. Although she suffered from a concussion, Picabo believes she came out of that crash a stronger, more confident skier. "I proved to myself I could wipe out without breaking something."

And she was right. At the Nagano Olympic games, she won an Olympic gold medal in the women's super-G race. But a speed skier's world is never without drama. "A month after winning the gold medal, I was in Switzerland skiing down a mountain when this fence got in my way!" She shattered her left leg and blew out her right knee. For a while during her recuperation, Picabo's natural, outgoing personality was hidden beneath a cloud of depression. She struggled to clear the fog and find her positive attitude.

Soon she took her own advice that she often would give to discouraged teammates: "Listen to yourself and listen to your body and you'll be okay. If you shoot high for your dreams, you'll have a long way to fall. The tough times teach you something. Face your fears and you'll be a better person because of it."

Discover Your Strength

Kathryn Reith
Vice President of Communications, Nike

There was no way she was going to be able to keep up with her college rowing team the next time they got together for a run. Kathryn was sure she couldn't jog more than 5 minutes before stomach cramps or breathing spasms would force her to quit. The day she joined her team for their run, Kathryn was worried she wouldn't be able to last the entire workout.

Somehow, Kathryn kept up the pace. When her teammates finally slowed to a stop, she asked how far they had run. Five miles! That was twice the distance she had ever run before! The next day, Kathryn's body was a little sore, but her confidence was stronger than ever. It dawned on her that she had capabilities she knew nothing about.

"When I was in high school, there were so few sports offered to girls, so I never really learned the rules, regulations, or the basic how-to's of playing sports. By the time I got to college, I didn't feel prepared enough to play. My confidence in my abilities was pretty low." Still, when Kathryn attended a freshmen orientation at Brown University, she saw the sign-up table for crew and thought it sounded cool. Being tall is an advantage in the sport of rowing, so the coach took one look at Kathryn's height and immediately signed her up.

"When I met the rest of my team, we found out none of us had ever touched an oar before!" So the women were evenly matched. But

Kathryn quickly progressed. Within months, she made it to the varsity team. While Kathryn's skills were becoming stronger, her team seemed to lag behind. "My coach put me in the 'stroke' position, which is the person who sets the pace and leads the boat. I would get so frustrated at my team for not going as fast as I knew we could."

During her summers, Kathryn rowed with other groups. The people she met in these rowing clubs gave her new appreciation and respect for what it means to work for a team. In the fall, as she returned to school and her college crew team, she found herself excited to meet up with her teammate buddies. "I came to see how everyone had something to contribute. We all have capabilities that make us fit together as a team. The best thing for me to do was not to wish they were somebody else but to figure out how we could all work best together."

In the working world, Kathryn can see how doing sports has made her more capable and confident. "After college, I did some volunteer work for the U.S. Rowing Association to help publicize their national championships. Next thing I knew, they hired me as their first Communications Director." Kathryn knew very little about doing the work her new job required. But her faith in herself was strong.

Now Kathryn is in charge of public relations for Nike. She makes sure all the interesting stories about Nike's women athletes are brought to the attention of newspapers, television reporters, and radio shows. Her job is heavy with responsibility, and she is in charge of many employees. Sometimes her job can be very stressful. "When I'm faced with a scary problem at work, I remember my crew coach who always told me I was more capable than I realized."

Giving Women's Sports a Place to Perform

Lydia Stephans

*Executive Producer of Sports Programming
for Oxygen Media and 1984 Olympic Speed Skating
Team Member*

When she was 6 years old, Lydia's grandmother moved in with her family. Instead of sitting by the fire knitting sweaters, this grand-mother spent her days in the backyard throwing fast pitches and curve balls to her granddaughter. Lydia's grandmother was a "bloomer girl"—from a professional, all-women baseball league that barnstormed the country while the men were away fighting in the second world war. "My grandmother was a true pioneer. She even taught me how to pitch a knuckleball," says Lydia.

When she was 12 years old, Lydia was watching the winter Olympics on television. She saw two women from her hometown win gold medals in a speed skating event. Something inside her clicked, and Lydia knew right then and there that she too was going to join the Olympic team as a speed skater. The fact that she had never even worn a pair of speed skates did not worry her one bit.

After only 4 years of speed skating, Lydia made it to the national championships. The first day of competition, she performed poorly. Even though there was still one more day to compete, people came up to Lydia saying how sorry they were that she did not have a chance to win, but there was always next year. Lydia could not believe they had already given up on her. Sure, a few miracles would have to happen, but there was still a chance she could win. The next day, Lydia's confidence and optimism paid off. She won the championship.

In 1984, Lydia's childhood dream came true when she made the Olympic speed skating team. She was the top American in the 1,000 meters and in the 100-meter "pack-style" race. Then, after graduating from Northwestern University, Lydia found herself working as a reporter for ABC sports covering the 1988 Winter Olympics in Calgary, Canada. Over the next few years, Lydia worked her way to the top and become the first woman Vice President for ABC Sports.

In 1999 Lydia was delighted to hear that ABC Sports was given the option to air the Women's World Cup Soccer games. The only problem was ABC's management was skeptical about the popularity of women's soccer, and did not believe there would be an audience for the games. Lydia was shocked. She pointed out that ABC aired the men's World Cup Soccer games even though the American team had little chance of winning. Yet the U.S. women's team were Olympic gold medalists and were favored to win the World Cup!

Lydia refused to give up and negotiated long and hard. Finally ABC agreed to share airing of the games with ESPN. For the championship game, USA versus China, more than half the televisions in the United States were tuned in to watch. Lydia remembers thinking to herself, "Okay, I wasn't a little nutty when I thought the World Cup was going to do so well!"

"After this, I came to realize that I followed women's sports with more passion than the people I worked with." So Lydia joined the new network Oxygen, as their Executive Producer of Sports Programming. "Girls, women, and men are demanding to see more women's sports on television and the internet. My job at Oxygen is to give women's sports the status it deserves." Just as her grandmother was a pioneer in women's sports, Lydia is too.

Fiery and Feminine

Sheryl Swoopes
Houston Comets, WNBA player and 1996 Olympic Gold Medalist

"Aw, let her shoot," one of the boys finally said. Sheryl easily caught the pass. The ball felt so good in her hands. Maybe she didn't want to shoot just yet. Now that the ball was hers, she was going to make the guys fight to get it back. Little did they know how skilled she had become. Sheryl knew this was her chance to show them what she had. When the guys saw how serious she was, they stopped being easy on her. Soon Sheryl was getting knocked to the ground, bruised, and banged up along with the rest of the guys on the court.

Now she had a new problem. "I thought if I played basketball good enough to beat the guys, they wouldn't like me anymore. I remember struggling with the dilemma of playing my best or slacking off just so they would include me." But Sheryl knew she loved playing basketball and she knew she was really good. So she decided to play the game the only way she knew how—tough and aggressive.

Playing basketball was Sheryl's favorite pastime, and that's all she thought it would ever be—just a hobby. So, as a young girl, Sheryl dreamed of one day being a Dallas cheerleader. "That was a job in sports I knew girls could do. I never saw or heard of a professional woman basketball player. But I knew everyone loved cheerleaders." But pom-poms and cheerleading outfits cost money that Sheryl's family could not spare. So she quickly gave up her dream of being a cheerleader and spent every free hour on the basketball court.

"My mom was a single parent of three kids, working several jobs to keep our family going. At first she didn't think I should take basketball so seriously. But she always encouraged us to be our best." Sheryl grew even more passionate about playing basketball. Soon she earned an athletic college scholarship, and eventually, the support of her mom. Today, her mother is Sheryl's number-one fan. Having her mom's encouragement made Sheryl realize just how important it is for parents to support their daughters in sports. "Sports, such as basketball, are not just for boys anymore. Girls should be told they can be feminine and fiery at the same time."

Besides her role as forward for the Houston Comets, Sheryl is first and foremost a mother. After her son Jordan was born, some people questioned whether or not Sheryl would ever be able to compete at her former level. "The negative comments got so bad, I too began to question my abilities." But once again, Sheryl proved her critics wrong.

Playing basketball is her profession and something she loves. But having the baby meant her body needed to get back into shape. Even on days when she felt tired or unmotivated, Sheryl forced herself into the gym. "I feel like I'm playing better than ever. My entire game is different. I improved my three-point shot, jump shot, my offense, and defense. I am so thankful and so glad that I stuck with it. And I believed in myself and never gave up."

Sports Resources
(listed alphabetically by sport)

Adventure Sports

Adventure Sports Online:
Rafting, Kayaking, Canoeing,
Backpacking
www.adventuresports.com

Archery

National Archery Association
One Olympic Plaza
Colorado Springs, Colorado 80909
Phone: (719) 578-4576
Fax: (719) 632-4733
e-mail: info@USArchery.org
Web: www.USArchery.org

National Field Archery Association
31407 Outer I-10
Redlands, California 92373
Phone: (909) 794-2133
Fax: (909) 794-8512
Web: www.smart.net/~stimsonr/
nfaafram.html

Badminton

U.S. Badminton Association
One Olympic Plaza/Bldg. 10/Room 1236
Colorado Springs, Colorado 80909
Phone: (719) 578-4808
Fax: (719) 578-4507
e-mail: usab@usabadminton.org
Web: www.usabadminton.org

Baseball

American Women's Baseball League
www.womenplayingbaseball.com

Little League Baseball Online
www.littleleague.org

Basketball

Amateur Athletic Union Girls Basketball
The Walt Disney World Resort
P.O. Box 10000
Lake Buena Vista, Florida 32823
Phone: (800) AAU-4USA
e-mail: eddie@aausports.org
Web: www.aausports.org

CBS Sports Line—Women's Basketball
www.sportsline.com/u/women/basketball

Women's National Basketball Association
www.wnba.com

Youth Basketball of America
10325 Orangewood Blvd.
Orlando, Florida 32821
Phone: (407) 363-9262
e-mail: yboahq@msn.com
Web: www.yboa.org

Bicycling

Bicycle Federation of America
1506 21st St. NW, Suite 200
Washington DC 20036
Phone: (202) 332-6986
Fax: (202) 463-6625
e-mail: bikefed@aol.com
Web: www.bikefed.org

USA Cycling
One Olympic Plaza
Colorado Springs, Colorado 80909
Phone: (719) 578-4581
Fax: (719) 578-4628
e-mail: usac@usacycling.org
Web: www.usacycling.org

American Bicycle Association—
Motorcross
www.ababmx.com

Billiards

Women's Professional Billiard Association
355 Lexington Ave., 17th Floor
New York, New York 10017-6603
Phone: (212) 297-2144
Fax: (212) 370-9047
e-mail: general_info@wpba.com
Web: www.WPBA.com

Billiards Congress of America
4345 Beverly St., Suite D
Colorado Springs, Colorado 80918
Phone: (719) 264-8300
Fax: (719) 264-0900
e-mail: program@coda.inav.net
Web: www.bca-pool.com

Bowling

The Women's International
Bowling Congress
5301 S. 76th St.
Greendale, Wisconsin 53129-1191
Phone: (414) 421-9000
Fax: (414) 421-4420
e-mail: ssavet@bowlinginc.com
Web: www.Bowl.com

Climbing

American Sports Climbing Federation
710 Tenth Street, Suite 130
Golden, Colorado 80401
Phone: (888) ASCFROX (main)
Fax: (212) 865-4383
e-mail: janesky@roguewave.com
Web: mindspring.com/~ascf

Diving

USA Diving
201 S. Capitol Ave., Suite 430
Indianapolis, Indiana 46225
Phone: (317) 237-5252
Fax: (317) 237-5257
e-mail: usdiving@aol.com
Web: www.usdiving.org

Fencing

U.S. Fencing Association
One Olympic Plaza
Colorado Springs, Colorado 80909
Phone: (719) 578-4511
Fax: (719) 632-5737
e-mail: USFencing@aol.com
Web: www.usfencing.org

Field Hockey

U.S. Field Hockey Association
One Olympic Plaza
Colorado Springs, Colorado 80909
Phone: (719) 578-4567
Fax: (719) 632-0979
e-mail: usfha@usfieldhockey.com
Web: www.usfieldhockey.com

Figure Skating

U.S. Figure Skating Association
20 First St.
Colorado Springs, Colorado 80906-5773
Phone: (719) 635-5200
Fax: (719) 635-9548
e-mail: USFSA1@aol.com
Web: www.usfsa.org

International Figure Skating Magazine
www.ifsmagazine.com

Football

U.S. Flag and Touch Football League
7709 Ohio Street
Mentor, Ohio 44060
Phone: (440) 974-8735
Fax: (440) 974-8735
e-mail: ustfl@aol.com
Web: www.e-.sports.com/ustfl.org

Golf

Ladies Professional Golf Association
100 International Golf Drive
Daytona Beach, Florida 32124
Phone: (904) 274-6200
Fax: (904) 274-1099
Web: www.lpga.com

U.S. Golf Association
P.O. Box 708
Far Hills, New Jersey 07931-0708
Phone: (908) 234-2300
Fax: (908) 234-9687
e-mail: usga@usga.org
Web: www.usga.org

Gymnastics

USA Gymnastics
Pan American Plaza
200 South Capital Ave., Suite 300
Indianapolis, Indiana 46225
Phone: (317) 237-5050
Fax: (317) 237-5069
Web: www.usa-gymnastics.org

U.S. Association of Independent
Gymnastics Clubs
235 Pinehurst Road
Wilmington, Delaware 19803
Phone: (302) 656-3706
Fax: (302) 656-8929
e-mail: USAIGC@delanet.com
Web: www.delanet.com/~usaigc

The Collegiate Gymnastics Info Center
www.troester.com/gym/

Hiking

American Hiking Society
1422 Fenwick Lane
Silver Spring, Maryland 20910
Phone: (301) 565-6704
Fax: (301) 565-6714
e-mail: info@americanhiking.org
Web: www.americanhiking.org

Hockey

USA Hockey
1775 Bob Johnson Drive
Colorado Springs, Colorado 80906
Phone: (719) 576-8724
Fax: (719) 538-1160
e-mail: usah@usahockey.org
Web: www.usahockey.com

U.S. Field Hockey Association
www.usfieldhockey.com

Women's Hockey Web
www.whockey.com

Horseback Riding

U.S. Equestrian Team
Pottersville Road
Gladstone, New Jersey 07934
Phone: (908) 234-1251
Fax: (908) 234-9417
Web: www.uset.com

American Horse Shows Association
4047 Iron Works Parkway
Lexington, Kentucky 40511
Phone: (606) 258-2472
Fax: (606) 231-6662
e-mail: N/A
Web: www.ahsa.org

Equestrian and Horse News
www.horsenet.com

In-Line Skating

International In-Line Skating Association
201 N. Front St. #306
Wilmington, New Jersey 28041
Phone: (910) 762-7004
Fax: (910) 762-9477
e-mail: director@iisa.org
Web: www.iisa.org

Jump Rope

U.S.A. Jump Rope Federation
www.usajrf.org

Lacrosse

U.S. Lacrosse
113 W. University Parkway
Baltimore, Maryland 21210
Phone: (410) 235-6982
Fax: (410) 366-6735
e-mail: info@lacrosse.org
Web: www.lacrosse.org

Martial Arts

U.S. Tae Kwan Do Union
One Olympic Plaza, Suite 405
Colorado Springs, Colorado 80909
Phone: (719) 578-4632
Fax: (719) 578-4642
e-mail: usakf@raex.com
Web: www.aakf.org

USA National Karate-Do Federation
P.O. Box 77083
Seattle, Washington 98177-7083
Phone: (206) 440-8386
Fax: (206) 367-7557
e-mail: karate@usankf.org
Web: www.usankf.org

Women Kickin It
19997 Stevens Creek Blvd., Suite #5
Cupertino, California 95014
Phone: (408) 873-0202
e-mail: women@womenkickinit.com
Web: www.womenkickinit.com/wki/contact.htm

U.S. Judo Association
21 North Union Blvd.
Colorado Springs, Colorado 80909
Phone: (719) 633-7750
Fax: (719) 633-4041
Web: www.csprings.com/usja

Paddling

U.S. Canoe and Kayak
P.O. Box 789
Lake Placid, New York 12946
Phone: (518) 523-1855
e-mail: USCKT@aol.com
Web: www.usacanoekayak.org

American Canoe Association
7432 Alban Station Blvd., Suite B-232
Springfield, Illinois 22150
Phone: (703) 451-0141
Fax: (703) 451-2245
e-mail: acadirect@aol.com
Web: www.aca-paddler.org

Racquetball

U.S. Racquet Association
1685 West Uintah
Colorado Springs, Colorado 80904-2921
Phone: (719) 635-5396
Fax: (719) 635-0685
e-mail: usragen@webaccess.net
Web: www.usra.org

Roller Skating

USA Roller Skating
4730 South St.
Lincoln, Nebraska 68506
Phone: (402) 483-7551
Fax: (402) 483-1465
e-mail: usacrs@usacrs.com
Web: www.usacrs.com

Roller Skating Association International
6905 Corporate Drive
Indianapolis, Indiana 46278
Phone: (317) 347-2626
Fax: (317) 347-2636
e-mail: rsa@rollerskating.org
Web: www.rollerskating.org

Rowing

U.S. Rowing Association
201 S. Capitol Ave., Suite 400
Indianapolis, Indiana 46225
Phone: (800) 314-4769
Fax: (317) 237-5646
e-mail: usrowing@aol.com
Web: www.usrowing.org

Running

Road Runners Clubs of America
1150 South Washington, Suite 250
Alexandria, Virginia 22314
Phone: (703) 836-0558
Fax: (703) 836-4430
e-mail: webmaster@rrca.org
Web: www.rrca.org

Skiing

U.S. Ski and Snowboard Association
1500 Kearns Blvd.
Bldg. F. Suite F200
Park City, Utah
Phone: (435) 649-9090
Fax: (435) 649-3613
e-mail: special2@ussa.org
Web: www.usskiteam.com

U.S. Collegiate Snowsport Association
314 W. Main St. #19
Kutztown, Pennsylvania 19530
Phone: (610) 683-0843
Fax: (610) 683-9870
e-mail: timl@uscsa.com
Web: www.uscsa.com

Winter Sports Foundation
P.O. Box 3710
Boulder, Colorado 80307-3710
Web: www.wintersports.org

Snowboarding

U.S. Amateur Snowboarding Association
www.usasa.org

Soccer

Women's Soccer Foundation
P.O. Box 600404
Newton, Massachusetts 02460
Phone: (617) 243-9487
Fax: (617) 243-0827
e-mail: webmaster@womensoccer.org
Web: www.womensoccer.org

U.S. Soccer Federation
1801-1811 South Prairie Avenue
Chicago, Illinois 60616
Phone: (312) 808-1300
Fax: (312) 808-1301
e-mail: socfed@aol.com
Web: www.us-soccer.com

High Tech Soccer
www.hightechsoccer.com/us.html

Soccer Times
www.soccertimes.com

Soccer Virginia
www.soccervirginia.com

Women's Soccer World Online
www.womensoccer.com

American Youth Soccer Association
www.soccer.org

Softball

Women's Pro Softball League
90 Madison Street, Suite 200
Denver, Colorado 80206
Phone: (303) 316-7800
Fax: (303) 316-2779
Web: www.prosoftball.com

USA Softball & Amateur
Softball Association
2801 NE 50th St.
Oklahoma City, Oklahoma 73111-7203
Phone: (405) 424-5266
Fax: (405) 424-3855
e-mail: bmccall@softball.org
Web: www.softball.org

Speedskating

Amateur Speedskating Union
1033 Shady Lane
Glen Ellyn, Illinois 60137
Phone: (630) 790-3230
Fax: (630) 790-3235
e-mail: ASUYates@aol.com
Web: http://www.speedskating.org

U.S. International
Speedskating Association
P.O. Box 450639
Westlake, Ohio 44145
Phone: (440) 899-0128
Fax: (440) 899-0109
e-mail: leo@roller-dome.com
Web: www.usspeedskating.org

Squash

U.S. Women's Intercollegiate Squash
Racquets Association
c/o Gail Ramsay, President
Fieldhouse Box 71, Jadwin Gym
Princeton, New Jersey 85444
Phone: (609) 258-5089
Fax: (609) 258-4477

U.S. Squash Racquets Association
P.O. Box 1216
Bala-Cynwyd, Pennsylvania 19004-1216
Phone: (610) 667-4006
Fax: (610) 667-6539
e-mail: ussquash@us-squash.org
Web: www.us-squash.org

SquashTalk
www. squashtalk.com

Surfing

Surfrider Foundation USA
122 S. El Camino Real #67
San Clemente, California 92672
Phone: (949) 492-8170
Fax: (949) 492-8142
e-mail: mbabski@surfrider.org
Web: www.surfrider.org

Swimming

SwimAmerica
2101 N. Andrews Ave. #107
Ft. Lauderdale, Florida 33311
Phone: (800) 356-2722
e-mail: swimamerica@usa.net
Web: swimamerica.org

USA Swimming
1 Olympic Plaza
Colorado Springs, Colorado 80909-5770
Phone: (719) 578-4578
Fax: (719) 578-4669
e-mail: ussinfo@usswim.org
Web: www.usswim.org

U.S. Synchronized Swimming
Pan American Plaza
201 S. Capitol Ave., Suite 901
Indianapolis, Indiana 46225
Phone: (317) 237-5700
Fax: (317) 237-5705
e-mail: webmaster@usasynchro.org
Web: www.usasynchro.org

Table Tennis

USA Table Tennis
One Olympic Plaza
Colorado Springs, Colorado 80909
Phone: (719) 578-4583
Fax: (719) 632-6071
e-mail: usatt@icx.net
Web: www.usatt.org

Tennis

U.S. Tennis Association
70 West Red Oak Lane
White Plains, New York 10604
Phone: (914) 696-7000
Fax: (914) 696-7167
e-mail: info@usta.com
Web: www.usta.com

Intercollegiate Tennis Association
www.tennisonline.com/ita

Track & Field

USA Track & Field
1 RCA Dome, Suite 140
Indianapolis, Indiana 46225
Phone: (317) 261-0500
Fax: (317) 261-0481
e-mail: mctrack@aol.com
Web: www.usatf.org

Volleyball

U.S. Volleyball Association
715 S. Circle Drive
Colorado Springs, Colorado 80910
Phone: (719) 228-6800
Fax: (719) 228-6899
e-mail: infor@usa~volleyball.org
Web: www.volleyball.org

U.S.A. Volleyball
www.usavolleyball.org

Water Polo

U.S. Water Polo
1685 West Uintah
Colorado Springs, Colorado 80904-2921
Phone: (719) 634-0699
Fax: (719) 634-0866
e-mail: uswpoffice@aol.com
Web: www.usawaterpolo.com

Women of Water Sports
5220 East Colonial Dr.
Orlando, Florida 32807
Phone: (407) 381-0024
e-mail: wowski@aol.com
Web: www.wowsports.org

Water Skiing
American Water Ski Association
799 Overlook Dr.
Winter Haven, Florida 33884-1671
Phone: (863) 324-4341
Fax: (863) 325-8259
e-mail: usawaterski@usawaterski.org
Web: www.usawaterski.org

Weight Lifting
National Strength and
Conditioning Association
1955 N. Union Blvd.
Colorado Springs, Colorado 80909
Phone: (800) 815-6826
Fax: (719) 632-6367
e-mail: ncsa@nsca-lift.org
Web: www.nsca-lift.org/menu.htm

Windsurfing
International Women's
Boardsailing Association
P.O. Box 116
Hood River, Oregon 97031
Phone: (503) 427-8566

U.S. Windsurfing Association
P.O. Box 978
Hood River, Oregon 97031
Phone: (809) 774-2796
Fax: (809) 774-2797
e-mail: USAW@aol.com
Web: www.windsurfer.com/uswa

Wrestling
USA Wrestling—
Women's Wrestling Committee
15418 S. 24th Street
Phoenix, Arizona 85044
Phone: (602) 759-4096

Yoga
U.S. Yoga Association
2159 Filbert
San Francisco, California 94123
Phone: (415) 931-YOGA
Fax: (415) 921-6676
e-mail: santonio@gateway.net
Web: www.usyoga.org

The American Yoga Association
P.O. Box 19986
Sarasota, Florida 34276
Phone: (941) 927-4977
Fax: (941) 921-9844
Web: americayoga association.org

Sources

Introduction

"Athletics in the Lives of Women and Girls."
http://www.feminist.org/research/sports6.html (1 February 2000).

"Women's Sports Facts." *Women's Sports Foundation*.
http://www.womenssportsfoundation.org (1 January 2000).

Chapter 2

Driscoll, Jim. "How to Build a Team from Scratch." *The Bergen Record*.
http://www.elibrary.com (9 October 1999).

O'Brien, Kathleen. "Camp Daze." *The Bergen Record*. http://www.elibrary.com
(26 March 1999).

Simons, Janet. "Camping It Up: There's a Summer Getaway for Every Kind of Kid for
Every Kind of Price." *Denver Rocky Mountain News*. http://www.elibrary.com
(24 December 1999).

Chapter 3

"Adolescents' Growth and Nutrition." *InteliHEALTH*.
http://www.intelihealth.com (1 December 1999).

Allen, Angela. "Help Girls Build Healthy Attitudes About Food." *The Columbian*.
http://www.elibrary.com (24 March 1998).

Atlas, Nava. Telephone interview. 1 December 1999.

"Calcium." *U.S. Department of Health and Human Services*.
http://www.health.org/gpower/AdultsWhoCare2/resources/
pubs/ComKit/index.htm (1 November 1999).

Christman, Vivian, R.D. Telephone interview. 1 December 1999.

Cummins, H.J. "Vegetarian Teens Can Reap Benefits." *Minneapolis-St. Paul Star
Tribune*. http://www.elibrary.com (21 October 1998).

"FDA Launches Calcium Education Pilot Campaign in Four States for Girls Aged 11–14."
Contemporary Women's Issues Database. http://www.elibrary.com (21 April 1997).

"Fitness and Bone Health." *American Dietetic Association*. http://www.eatright.org
(1 November 1999).

"Fitness and Healthful Eating for Children." *American Dietetic Association*.
http://www.eatright.org (1 November 1999).

"The Food Guide Pyramid." http://www.kidshealth.org (1 February 2000).

Greggains, Joanie. Telephone interview. 8 September 1999.

Greggains, Joanie and Patricia Romanowski. *Fit Happens*. New York: Random House, 2000.

Ireland, Corydon. "Author Proves 'Vegetables Rock' To Teenagers." *Gannett News Service*. http://www.elibrary.com (16 March 1999).

"Less Sugar, Less You." http://www.fitteen.com (1 November 1999).

Lewis, Bea. "Good For You." *Newsday*. http://www.elibrary.com (5 May 1999).

Mack, Patricia. "Eating to Win—For Athletes, It All Starts with Balance," *The Bergen Record*. http://www.elibrary.com (24 June 1992).

"Make Fitness Fun for Kids!" *American Dietetic Association*. http://www.eatright.org (1 November 1999).

Mangels, Reed, R.D., Ph.D. Telephone interview. 1 December 1999.

"Nutrition Fuels Fitness: Let's Get Moving!" *The American Dietetic Association*. http://www.eatright.org (1 November 1999).

Rinzler, Carol Ann. *Nutrition for Dummies*. Foster City: IDG Books Worldwide, 1999.

Roblin, Lynn. "Eat Right: Teens Need Healthy Food, Active Living." *Toronto Star*. http://www.elibrary.com (26 May 1999).

"School-Age Children Growth & Nutrition." *InteliHEALTH*. http://www.intelihealth.com (1 November 1999).

Schwager, Tina and Michele Schuerger. *All The Right Moves: A Girl's Guide to Getting Fit and Feeling Good*. Minneapolis: Freespirit Publishing, 1998.

"U.S. Teenage Girls Missing Out on Calcium." *Reuters*. http://www.elibrary.com (14 January 1997).

"Vegetarian Teens." *American Dietetic Association*. http://www.eatright.org (1 November 1999).

Chapter 4

Bellaby, Mara. "Study: Girl Smokers More Likely to Be Overweight." *Associated Press Online*. http://www.elibrary.com (3 August 1998).

"Children's Sedentary Lifestyle: A Forerunner of Unhealthy Adulthood." *USA Today Magazine*. http://www.elibrary.com (1 May 1998).

Cummins, H.J. "Study: Teen Girls Not Making Great Choices." *Star Tribune*. http://www.elibrary.com (1 November 1999).

Emery, Gene. "Girls' Lungs More Sensitive to Smoking." *Reuters*. http://www.elibrary.com (25 September 1999).

Ignico, Arlene. "Exercise." http://www.fitteen.com/exercise.html (5 January 2000).

Kauchak, Theresa. *Good Sports*. Minneapolis: Pleasant Company, 1999.

Leesa, Christina. *Women Who Win*. New York: Universe Publishing, 1998.

Loosli, Alvin, M.D. Telephone interview. 13 December 1999.

"NOT on Tobacco: A Total Health Approach to Helping Teens Stop Smoking." *American Lung Association of Oregon*. http://www.lungoregon.org/NOT.htm (6 March 2000).

Ochs, Ridgely. "Schooling Teens on the Right Path to a Healthier Life." *Newsday*. http://www.elibrary.com (14 April 1998).

Painter, Kim. "Start to Exercise at a Young Age—But Don't Overdo It." *USA Today*. http://www.elibrary.com (19 July 1994).

Rathbun, Mickey. "Features: Play It Safe!" *Sports Illustrated For Kids*. http://www.elibrary.com (1 May 1998).

Thompson, Damon. "Defending Your Goals!" *The Nemours Foundation*. http://www.KidsHealth.org (1 November 1999).

"Why Exercise Is Wise." *The American Dietetic Association*. http://www.eatright.org (1 November 1999).

Chapter 5

King, Paula, M.D. "Mental Coaches Can Enhance Good Game." *The Arizona Republic*. http://www.elibrary.com (14 August 1998).

Rasmusson, Erika. "I Think I Can, I Think I Can." *Sports Illustrated for Women*. Fall 1999: 43–44.

Savoy, Carolyn and Patricia Beitel. "The Relative Effect of a Group and Group/Individualized Program on State Anxiety and State Self-Confidence." *Journal of Sport Behavior*. http://www.elibrary.com (1 September 1997).

Strasser, Teresa. "Berkeley Author-Therapist Leading Mental Workouts." *Northern California Jewish Bulletin*. http://www.elibrary.com (26 May 1995).

Chapter 6

Buzby, Jonathan H. "Parents' Perspectives: Taking the Fun Out of Play." http://www.chre.vt.edu/fs/rstratto/CYSarchive/FeatureJan98.html (9 January 2000).

Crary, David. "Parents: Be Wary of Grooming Sports Stars." *Minneapolis Star Tribune*. http://www.elibrary.com (6 November 1999).

Creager, Ellen. "Understanding Why and When Kids Drop Out of Sports." *The Dallas Morning News*. http://www.elibrary.com (24 August 1999).

Legarza, Mike. *The Arete Peninsula Basketball Association Handbook*. San Francisco: The Arete Peninsula Basketball Association, 1999.

Lieberman-Cline, Nancy. "Coaches Who Lose Composure Set Poor Example." *The Dallas Morning News*. http://www.elibrary.com (9 January 1997).

Wooldridge, Tracie. "Coaching Motivation for Females." http://www.chre.vt.edu/fs/rstratto/CYSarchive/FeatureJan98.html (9 January 2000).

Chapter 7

Anderson, Kelli, Dimity McDowell, and Ivan Maisel. "Head of the Class." *Sports Illustrated For Women*. http://www.elibrary.com (1 November 1999).

"Athletic Sports Scholarships at U.S. Colleges and Universities." http://www.ftclondon.co.uk/athsch.htm (9 January 2000).

"Career Choices: A Resource Guide." http://www.melpomene.org (9 January 2000).

Gummer, Scott. "How to Get into College." *USA Weekend*. 14–16 January 2000: p. 13–16.

Herman, Steve. "Women Show Continued Gains in Sports Participation, Scholarships." *San Francisco Examiner*. 26 October 1999.

Chapter 8

Gebhardt, Sarah. Telephone interview. 5 November 1999.

Granato, Cammi. Telephone interview. 22 May 1998.

"Jade Smalls, Miss Illinois." http://www.missamerica.org/1999/il.html (1 September 1999).

Lopiano, Donna. Telephone interview. 22 May 1998.

Meyer, John. "Street Smart: Picabo Learns from Crash Test, Earns Gold." *Rocky Mountain News*. http://www.elibrary.com (13 February 1998).

Moore, David. "One Big, Happy Family Street Toughs it Out Through Peaks, Valleys." *USA Today*. http://www.elibrary.com (27 November 1996).

"Picabo Street Recovers From Depression." *ABC Good Morning America*. http://www.elibrary.com (25 February 1999).

Reed, Susan and Tom Cunneff. "Jocks: Norway, Her Way: As Mischievous as Her Name, Idaho's Picabo." *People*. http://www.elibrary.com (7 February 1994).

Reith, Kathryn. Telephone interview. 20 November 1999.

Richardson, Dot. Telephone interview. 1 June 1998.

Smalls, Jade. Telephone interview. 1 October 1999.

Stevens, Lydia. Telephone interview. 22 December 1999.

Street, Picabo. Telephone interview by Marianne Monson-Burton. 15 June 1999.

Swoopes, Sheryl. Telephone interview. 7 March 2000.

Visser, Lesley. Telephone interview. 1 November 1999.

Glossary

amenorrhea: the absence of menstruation, which can sometimes be caused by poor nutrition.

anorexia nervosa: an eating disorder often brought about by fear of weight gain, and leading to faulty eating patterns, excessive weight loss, and malnutrition.

biceps: the large muscle in the front of the upper arm.

bulimia: an eating disorder marked by a constant craving for food, and which can lead to bingeing and purging.

calcium: a nutritious element, found in dairy and substitute dairy products, one of the benefits of which is keeping bones strong and healthy.

carbohydrates: compounds composed of carbon, hydrogen, and oxygen that produce energy when consumed. The body burns simple carbohydrates rapidly. They are found in sugar products. Complex carbohydrates, which the body burns more slowly, can be found in foods that are high in starch, such as potatoes, pasta, and bread.

diuretic: a chemical compound that depletes the body's fluids and its ability to retain fluids.

electrolytes: non-metallic ionic conductors that carry energy through the body.

equestrian: having to do with horses; a horseback rider.

glucose: the form of sugar that carbohydrates take when digested.

glycogen: the form of sugar that carbohydrates take when they are stored in the body.

intravenous tube: a tube that transports liquids into the body through a needle that is inserted into a vein.

javelin: a lightweight spear thrown in track and field events.

kayak: a type of canoe that has a small opening for only one person.

metabolism: the process by which food is changed into energy and body tissue, and then disposed of as waste.

osteoporosis: a condition characterized by a decrease in bone mass due to the depletion of calcium, making the bones brittle and more breakable.

potassium: a metallic element that occurs in nature. Eating foods rich in this element can help eliminate muscle cramps.

psyche: (v) to mentally prepare for a performance, competition, or other situation or event; to anticipate with enthusiasm.

quadriceps: the muscle that extends down the front of the thigh.

triathlete: an athlete who participates in conferences and meets that require completion of a course combining at least three sports, usually swimming, cross-country, and bicycling.

zinc: A metallic element that occurs in many minerals and is an essential nutrient for both plants and animals.

Index

aerobics 61, 62, 63
archery 21

badminton 11
baseball 26, 31, 82, 104, 129, 130, 133
basketball 7, 8, 11, 13, 25, 27, 31, 33, 67,
   94, 97, 98, 102, 104, 114, 122, 131, 132,
   143, 144
biking 10, 11, 21
billiards 11, 19, 21
bowling 11, 19, 21, 27, 33

calcium 43, 44, 45, 51, 52
canoeing 21
careers 110, 114, 115, 116, 117, 118, 119, 120,
   121, 122
coaches 98, 99, 100, 101, 102

dancing 21, 25, 99
diving 19, 22, 126

eating disorders 52, 53

fat 47, 52, 53
fencing 22, 34
fiber 42, 52
food pyramid 40, 41, 42, 43, 44, 46
football 31, 104

golf 19, 80, 81
gymnastics 19, 22, 48, 69, 94, 105

hiking 10, 11, 22
hockey 7, 19, 31, 103, 104, 127, 128, 135, 136
horseback riding 22, 25, 32, 80
hydration 49, 50, 51

injuries 56, 57, 68, 69

javelin 24
jump rope 94

lacrosse 31

martial arts 16, 19, 23, 24, 76, 78, 114, 122

Olympics 28, 128, 134, 137, 138, 141, 142,
   143, 144

protein 45, 51, 52

racquetball 23
relaxation 76, 77
rock climbing 11, 12, 20, 21
rowing 19, 139, 140
rugby 31
running 29, 69, 78, 102, 139

scholarships 7, 8, 110, 112, 113, 114
scuba diving 10
self-talk 82, 83
skating 11, 22, 23, 32, 141, 142
skiing 10, 11, 19, 21, 22, 24, 80, 81, 137, 138
smoking 15, 70, 71, 72
snowboarding 10, 11, 23
soccer 7, 11, 12, 13, 31, 32, 33, 47, 48, 69,
   70, 77, 84, 85, 98, 104, 105, 114, 122
softball 6, 13, 27, 31, 33, 67, 69, 77, 97, 98,
   114, 122, 130, 133, 134
squash 23
strength training 64, 65, 66, 67
stretching 58, 59, 60, 61
surfing 8, 11, 15, 20, 34, 125, 126
swimming 11, 13, 14, 19, 23, 69

target heart rate 61, 62
tennis 11, 23, 25, 94, 99
track and field 19, 24, 25, 79, 98, 102
training 20, 29
triathlete 29, 79
tryouts 28, 29
tumbling 120

vitamins 47
volleyball 31, 67, 82, 85, 99, 120

water polo 27, 32
windsurfing 24
wrestling 24

yoga 24, 77